The Quest Of The Simple Life

By

William James Dawson

CHAPTER I

THE HOUSE OF BONDAGE

For a considerable number of years I had been a resident in London, which city I regarded alternately as my Paradise and my House of Bondage. I am by no means one of those who are always ready to fling opprobrious epithets at London, such as 'a pestilent wen,' a cluster of 'squalid villages,' and the like; on the contrary, I regard London as the most fascinating of all cities, with the one exception of that city of Eternal Memories beside the Tiber. But even Horace loved the olive-groves of Tivoli more than the far-ranged splendours of the Palatine; and I may be pardoned if an occasional vision of green fields often left my eye insensitive to metropolitan attractions.

This is a somewhat sonorous preface to the small matter of my story; but I am anxious to elaborate it a little, lest it should be imagined that I am merely a person of bucolic mind, to whom all cities or large congregations of my fellow-men are in themselves abhorrent. On the contrary I have an inherent love of all cities which are something more than mere centres of manufacturing industry. The truly admirable city secures interest, and even passionate love, not because it is a congeries of thriving factories, but rather by the dignity of its position, the splendour of its architecture, the variety and volume of its life, the imperial, literary, and artistic interests of which it is the centre, and the prolongation of its history through tumultuous periods of time, which fade into the suggestive shadows of antiquity. London answers perfectly to this definition of the truly admirable city. It has been the stage of innumerable historic pageants; it presents an unexampled variety of life; and there is majesty in the mere sense of multitude with which it arrests and often overpowers the mind.

As I have already, with an innocent impertinence, justified myself by Horace, so I will now justify myself by Wordsworth, whose famous sonnet written on Westminster Bridge is sufficient proof that he could feel the charm of cities as deeply as the charm of Nature. 'Earth hath not anything to show more fair,' wrote Wordsworth, and of a truth London has moods and moments of almost unearthly beauty, perhaps unparalleled by any vision that inebriates the eye in the most gorgeous dawn that flushes Alpine snows, or the most solemn sunset that builds a gate of gold across the profound depth of Borrowdale or Wastwater. He who has seen the tower of St. Clement Danes swim up, like an insubstantial fabric, through violet mist above the roaring Strand; or the golden Cross upon St. Paul's with a flag of tinted cloud flying from it; or the solemn reaches of the Thames bathed in smoky purple at the slow close of a summer's day, will know what I mean, and will (it is possible) have some memory of his own which will endorse the justness of my praise.

From this exalted prelude I will at once descend to more prosaic matter, leaving my reader, in his charity, to devise for me an apology which I have neither the wit nor the desire to invent for myself. With the best will in the world to speak in praise of cities it must be owned that the epic and lyric moments of London are infrequent. As a casual resident in London, a student and spectator, free to leave it when I willed, I could have been heartily content; but I, in common with some insignificant millions of my fellow-creatures, was bound to live in London as a means of living at all. He is no true citizen who merely comes up to town 'for the season,' alternating the pleasures of town with those of the country; he alone is the true citizen who *must* live amid the roar of the street all the year round, and for years together. If I could choose for myself I would even now choose the life of pleasant alternation between town and country, because I am persuaded that the true piquancy and zest of all pleasures lies in contrast. But fate orders these things for us, and takes no account of our desires, unless it be to treat them with habitual irony. At five-and-twenty the plain fact met me—that I must needs live in London, because my bread could be earned nowhere else. No choice was permitted me; I must go where crowds were, because from the favour or necessities of such crowds I must gather the scanty tithes which put food upon my table and clothes upon my back. When eminent writers, seated at ample desks, from which they command fair views of open country, denounce with prophetic fervour the perils which attend the growth of cities, they somewhat overlook the fact that the growth of cities is a sequence, alike ineluctable and pitiless, of the modern struggle for existence. One cannot be a lawyer, or a banker, a physician or a journalist, without neighbours. He can scarce be a literary man in perfect sylvan solitude, unless his work is of such quality—perhaps I should have said such popularity—that it wins for him immediate payment, or unless his private fortune be such that he can pursue his aims as a writer with entire indifference to the half-yearly statements of his publisher. In respect of the various employments of trade and commerce, the case is still plainer. Men must needs go where the best wages may be earned; and under modern conditions of life it is as natural that population should flow toward cities, as that rivers should seek the sea. These matters will be more particularly discussed later on; it is enough for me to explain at present that I was one of those persons for whom life in a city was an absolute necessity.

It is not until one is tied to a locality that its defects become apparent. A street that interests the mind by some charm of populous vivacity when it is traversed at random and without object, becomes inexpressibly wearisome when it is the thoroughfare of daily duty. My daily duty took me through a long stretch of Oxford Street, which is a street not altogether destitute of some real claim to gaiety and dignity. At first I was ready to concede this claim, and even to endorse it with enthusiasm; but from the day when I realised that Oxford Street conducted me, by a force of inevitable gravitation, to a desk in an office, I began to loathe it. The eye became conscious of a hundred defects and incongruities; the tall houses rose like prison walls; the resounding tumult of the streets seemed like the clamour of tormented spirits. For the first time I began to understand why imaginative writers had often likened London to Inferno.

I well remember by what a series of curious expedients I endeavoured to evade these sensations. The most obvious was altogether to avoid this glittering and detested thoroughfare by making long detours through the meaner streets which lay behind it; but this was merely to exchange one kind of aesthetic misery which had some alleviations for another kind which had none. Sometimes I endeavoured to contrive a doubtful exhilaration from the contrast which these meaner streets afforded; saying to myself, as I pushed my way through the costers' stalls of Great James Street, 'Now you are exchanging squalor for magnificence. Be prepared for a surprise.' But the ruse failed utterly, and my mind laughed aloud at the pitiful imposture. Another device was to create points of interest, like a series of shrines along a tedious road, which should present some aspect of allurement. There was a book-shop here or an art-shop there; yesterday a biography of Napoleon was exhibited in the one, or a print of Murillo's 'Flight into Egypt,' in the other; and it is become a matter of speculation whether they were there to-day. Just as a solitary sailor will beguile the tedium of empty days at sea by a kind of cribbage, in which the left hand plays against the right, so I laid odds for and against myself on such trifles as these, and even went so far as to keep an account of my successes and my failures. Thus, for a whole month I was interested in a person quite unknown to me, who wore an obsolete white beaver hat, appeared punctually at the corner of Bond Street at half-past five in the afternoon, and spent half an hour in turning over the odd volumes displayed on the street board of a secondhand-book shop not far from Oxford Circus. His appearances were so planetary in their regularity that one might have reckoned time by them. Who he was, or what his objects in life may have been, I never learned. I never saw him walk but in the one direction; I never saw him buy one of the many books which he examined: perhaps he also was afflicted with the tedium of London, and took this singular way of getting through a portion of his sterile day with a simulated interest. At all events he afforded me an interest, and when he vanished at the end of the month, Oxford Street once more became intolerable to me.

These particulars appear so foolish and so trivial that most persons will find them ridiculous, and even the most sympathetic will perhaps wonder why they are recorded. They were, however, far from trivial to me. The marooned seaman saves his sanity by cutting notches in a stick, the solitary prisoner by friendship with a mouse; and when life is reduced to the last exiguity of narrowness, the interests of life will be narrow too. No writer, whose work is familiar to me, has ever yet described with unsparing fidelity the kind of misery which lies in having to do precisely the same things at the same hour, through long and consecutive periods of time. The hours then become a dead weight which oppresses the spirit to the point of torture. Life itself resembles those dreadful dreams of childhood, in which we see the ceiling and the walls of the room contract round one's helpless and immobile form. Blessed is he who has variety in his life: thrice blessed is he who has both freedom and variety: but the subordinate toiler in the vast mechanism of a great city has neither. He will sit at the same desk, gaze upon the same unending rows of figures, do, in fact, the same things year in and year out till his youth has withered into age. He himself becomes little better than a mechanism. There is no form of outdoor employment of which this can be said. The life of the agricultural labourer, so often pitied for its monotony, is variety itself compared with the life of the commercial clerk. The labourer's tasks are at least changed by the seasons; but time brings no such diversion to the clerk. It is this horrible monotony which so often makes the clerk a foul-minded creature; driven in upon himself, he has to create some kind of drama for his instincts and imaginations, and often from the sorriest material. When I played single-handed cribbage with the few trivial interests which I knew, I at least took an innocent diversion; and I may claim that my absurd fancies injured no one, and were certainly of some service to myself.

The outsider usually imagines that great cities afford unusual opportunities of social intercourse, and when I first became a citizen I found this prospect enchanting. I scanned the horizon eagerly for these troops of friends which a city was supposed to furnish: quested here and there for a responsive pair of eyes; made timid approaches which were repulsed; and, finally, after much experiment, had to admit that the whole idea was a delusion. No doubt it is true enough that, with a settled and considerable income, and the power of entertaining, friends are to be found in plenty. But Grosvenor Square and Kentish Town do not so much as share a common atmosphere. In the one it is a pleasant tradition that the house door should be set wide to all comers who can contribute anything to the common social stock; in the other, the house door is jealously locked and barred. The London clerk does not care to reveal the shifts and the bareness of his domestic life. He will reside in one locality for years without so much as seeking to know his next-door neighbour. He will live on cordial terms with his comrade in the office, but will never dream of inviting him to his home. His instinct of privacy is so abnormal that it becomes mere churlishness. His wife, if he have one, usually fosters this spirit for reasons of her own. Her interests end with the clothing and education of her children. She does not wish for friends, does not cultivate the grace of hospitality, and is indifferent to social intercourse. In short, the barbaric legend that an Englishman's house is his castle, is nowhere so much respected as in London.

The exhausting character of life in London, and the mere vastness of its geographical area, do something to produce this result. Men who leave home early in the morning, sit for many hours in an office, and reach home late at night, soon lose both the instinct and desire for social intercourse. They prefer the comfortable torpor of the fireside. If some imperative need of new interests torments them, they seek relaxation in the music-hall or some other place of popular resort. The art of conversation is almost extinct in a certain type of Londoner. He knows nothing to converse about outside his business interests, his family concerns, and perhaps the latest sensation of the daily newspaper. Those lighter flights of fancy, those delicate innuendoes and allusions of implied experience or culture—all the give-and-take of happily contending minds—all, indeed, that makes true conversation—is a science utterly unknown to him. A certain superficial nimbleness of mind he does sometimes possess, but for all that he is a dull creature, made dull by the limitations of his life.

If it should happen, as it often may, that such a man has some genuine instinct for friendship, and has a friend to whom he can confide his real thoughts, the chances are that his friend will be separated from him by the mere vastness of London. To the rural mind the metropolis appears an entity; in reality it is an empire. A journey from the extreme north to the extreme south, from Muswell Hill to Dulwich, is less easily accomplished, and often less speedily, than a journey from London to Birmingham. There is none of that pleasant 'dropping-in' for an evening which is possible in country towns of not immoderate radius. Time-tables have to be consulted, engagement-books scanned, serious preparations made, with the poor result, perhaps, of two hours' hurried intercourse. The heartiest friendship does not long survive this malignity of circumstance. It is something to know that you have a friend, obscurely hidden in some corner of the metropolis; but you see him so rarely, that when you meet, it is like forming a new friendship rather than pursuing an old one. It is little wonder that, under such conditions, visits grow more and more infrequent, and at last cease. A message at Christmas, an intimation of a birth, a funeral card, are the solitary relics and mementoes of many a city friendship not extinct, but utterly suspended.

I dwell on these obvious characteristics of London life, because in course of time they assumed for me almost terrifying dimensions. After ten years of arduous toil I found myself at thirty-five lonely, friendless, and imprisoned in a groove of iron, whose long curves swept on inevitably to that grim terminus where all men arrive at last. Sometimes I chided myself for my discontent; and certainly there were many who might have envied me. I occupied a fairly comfortable house in a decayed terrace where each house was exactly like its neighbour, and had I told any one that the mere aspect of this grey terrace oppressed me by its featureless monotony, I should have been laughed at for my pains. I believe that I was trusted by my employers, and if a mere automatic diligence can be accounted a virtue, I merited their trust. In course of time my income would have been increased, though never to that degree which means competence or freedom. To this common object of ambition I had indeed long ago become indifferent. What can a few extra pounds a year bring to a man who finds himself bound to the same tasks, and those tasks distasteful? I was married and had two children; and the most distressing thought of all was that I saw my children predestined to the same fate. I saw them growing up in complete destitution of those country sights and sounds which had made my own youth delightful; acquiring the superficial sharpness of the city child and his slang; suffering at times by the anaemia and listlessness bred of vitiated air; high-strung and sensitive as those must needs be whose nerves are in perpetual agitation; and when, in chance excursions to the country, I compared my children with the children of cottagers and ploughmen, I felt that I had wronged them, I saw my children foredoomed, by an inexorable destiny, to a life at all points similar with my own. In course of time they also would become recruits in the narrow-chested, black-coated army of those who sit at desks. They would become slaves without having known the value of freedom; slaves not by capture but by heritage. More and more the thought began to gather shape, Was I getting the most, or the best, out of life? Was there no other kind of life in which toil was redeemed from baseness by its own inherent interest, no life which offered more of tranquil satisfaction and available, if humble, happiness? Day by day this thought sounded through my mind, and each fresh discouragement and disability of the life I led gave it sharper emphasis. At last the time came when I found an answer to it, and these chapters tell the story of my seeking and my finding.

CHAPTER II

GETTING THE BEST OUT OF LIFE

The reader will perhaps say that the kind of miseries recounted in the previous chapter are more imaginary than real. Many thousands of people subsist in London upon narrow means, and do not find the life intolerable. They have their interests and pleasures, meagre enough when judged by a superior standard, but sufficient to maintain in them some of the vivacity of existence. No doubt this is true. I remember being struck some years ago by the remark of a person of distinction, equally acquainted with social life in its highest and its lowest forms. Mr. H., as I will call this person, said that the dismal pictures drawn by social novelists of life among the very poor were true in fact, but wrong in perspective. Novelists described what their own feelings would be if they were condemned to live the life of the disinherited city drudge, rather than the actual feelings of the drudge himself. A man of education, accustomed to easy means, would suffer tortures unspeakable if he were made to live in a single room of a populous and squalid tenement, and had to subsist upon a wage at once niggardly and precarious. He would be tormented with that memory of happier things, which we are told is a 'sorrow's crown of sorrow.' But the man who has known no other condition of life is unconscious of its misery. He has no standard of comparison. An environment which would drive a man of refinement to thoughts of suicide, does not produce so much as dissatisfaction in him. Hence there is far more happiness among the poor than we imagine. They see nothing deplorable in a lot to which they have become accustomed; they are as our first parents before their eyes were opened to a knowledge of good or evil; or, to take a less mythical illustration, they are as the contented savage, to whom the refinements of European civilisation are objects of ridicule rather than envy.

I quote this opinion for what it is worth; but it has little relevance to my own case. I am the only competent judge of my own feelings. I know perfectly well that these feelings were not shared by men who shared the conditions of my own life. There was a clerk in the same office with me who may be taken as an example of his class. Poor Arrowsmith—how well I recall him!—was a little pallid man, always neatly if shabbily dressed, punctual as a clock, and of irreproachable diligence. He was verging on forty, had a wife and family whom I never saw, and an aged mother whom he was proud to support. He was of quite imperturbable cheerfulness, delighted in small jokes, and would chatter like a daw when occasion served him. He had never read a book in his life; his mind subsisted wholly upon the halfpenny newspapers. He had no pleasures, unless one can count as such certain Bank Holiday excursions to Hampstead Heath, which were performed under a heavy sense of duty to his family. He had lived in London all his days, but knew much less of it than the country excursionist. He had never visited St. Paul's or Westminster Abbey; had never travelled so far as Kew or Greenwich; had never been inside a picture gallery; and had never attended a concert in his life. The pendulum of his innocuous existence swung between the office and his home with a uniform monotony. Yet not only was he contented with his life, but I believe that he regarded it as entirely successful. He had counted it a great piece of luck when he had entered the office as a youth of sixteen, and the glow of his good fortune still lingered in his mind at forty. He regarded his employers with a species of admiring awe not always accorded to kings. The most violent social democrat could have made nothing of Arrowsmith; there was not the least crevice in his heart in which the seed of discontent could have found a lodgment. As for making any question of whether he was getting the best or most out of life, Arrowsmith was as incapable as a kitten.

The virtues of Arrowsmith, which were in their way quietly heroic, impressed me a good deal; but his abject contentment with the limitations of his lot appalled me. I felt a dread grow in me lest I should become subdued to the element in which I worked as he was. I asked myself whether a life so destitute of real interests and pleasures was life at all? I made fugitive attempts to allure the little man into some realms of wider interest, but with the most discouraging results. I once insisted on taking him with me for a day in Epping Forest. He came reluctantly, for he did not like leaving his wife at home, and it seemed that no persuasion could induce her to undertake so adventurous a jaunt. He was no walker, and half a dozen miles along the Forest roads tired him out. By the afternoon even his cheerfulness had vanished; he gazed with blank and gloomy eyes upon the wide spaces of the woodland scenery. He did not regain his spirits till we drew near Stratford on the homeward journey. At the first sight of gas-lit streets he brightened up, and I am persuaded that the rancid odours of the factories at Bow were sweeter in his nostrils than all the Forest fragrances. I never asked him again to share a pleasure for which I now perceived he had no faculty; but I often asked myself how long it would take for a city life to extirpate in me the taste by which Nature is appreciated, as it had in Arrowsmith.

I have taken Arrowsmith as an example of the narrowness of interest created by a city life, and it would be easy to offer an apology for him, which I, for one, would most heartily endorse. The poor fellow was very much the creature of his circumstances. But this was scarcely the case with another man I knew, whose circumstances, had he known how to use them, might have afforded him the opportunity of many cultivated tastes. He was the son of a small farmer, born in the same village as myself. By some curious accident he was flung into the vortex of London life at seventeen, and became a clerk in a reputable firm of stockbrokers in Throgmorton Street. He rose rapidly, speculated largely and successfully for himself, became a partner, and was rich at thirty. I used to meet him occasionally, for he never forgot that we had sat upon the same bench at school. I can see him still; well-fleshed and immaculately dressed; his waistcoat pockets full of gold; a prop of music-halls, a patron of expensive restaurants; flashing from one to the other in the evening hours in swift hansoms; a man envied and admired by a host of clerks in Throgmorton Street to whom he appeared a kind of Napoleon of finance. I will confess that I myself was a little dazzled by his careless opulence. When he took me to dine with him he thought nothing of giving the head waiter a sovereign as a guarantee of careful service, or of sending another sovereign to the master of the orchestra with a request for some particular piece of music which he fancied. He once confided to me that he had brought off certain operations which had made him the possessor of eighty thousand pounds. To me the sum seemed immense, but he regarded it as a bagatelle. When I suggested certain uses for it, such as retirement to the country, the building of a country house, the collection of pictures or of a library, he laughed at me. He informed me that he never spent more than a single day in the country every year; it was spent in visiting his father at the old farm. He loathed the quiet of the country, and counted his one day in the year an infliction and a sacrifice. Books and pictures he had cared for once, but as he now put it, he had 'no use for them.' It seemed that all his eighty thousand pounds was destined to be flung upon the great roulette table of stock and share speculations. It was not that he was avaricious; few men cared less for money in itself; but he could not live without the excitement of speculation. 'I prefer the air of Throgmorton Street to any air in the world,' he observed. 'I am unhappy if I leave it for a day.' So far as knowledge of or interest in

London went, he was not a whit better than poor shabby Arrowsmith. His London stretched no further than from the Bank to Oxford Circus, and the landmarks by which he knew it were restaurants and music-halls.

The man seemed so satisfied with everything about his life that it was a kind of joy to meet him. The sourness of my own discontent was dissolved in the alembic of his joviality. Yet it was certain that he lived a life of the most torturing anxiety. There were recurring periods when his fortune hung in the balance, and his financial salvation was achieved as by fire. When he sat silent for a moment, strange things were written on his face. Haggard lines ran across the brow; the hollows underneath the eyes grew deep; and one could see that black care sat upon his shoulders. There was a listening posture of the head, as of one apprehensive of the footfall of disaster, and though he was barely forty, his hair was white. What happened to him finally I do not know. I missed him for a year or two; inquired at the hotel where he had lived and found him gone; and I thought I read in the sarcastic smile of the hotel-manager more knowledge than he was willing to communicate. I imagine that he went down in some financial storm, like ships at sea that are heard of no more; the Napoleon of finance had somewhere found his Waterloo. The reflection is inevitable; what had he got out of life after all? He had won neither peace nor honour; he had known nothing of the finer joys or tastes; he had enjoyed no satisfying pleasures; such triumph as he had known had been the brief triumph of the gambler. Upon the whole I thought the narrow tedious life of Arrowsmith the worthier.

Reflections of this nature are usually attributed to mere envy or contempt of wealth, which is a temper not less sordid than a love of wealth. For my part I can but profess that I feel for wealth neither envy nor contempt. On the contrary, I love to imagine myself wealthy, and I flatter myself—as most poor men do—that I am a person peculiarly fitted by nature to afford a conspicuous example of how wealth should be employed. I like to dramatise my fancies, and the more impossible these fancies are, the more convincing is the drama that can be educed from them. Thus I have several times built palaces which have rivalled the splendours of the Medici; I have administered great estates to the entire satisfaction of my tenants; I have established myself as the Maecenas of art and literature; and were I ever called to play these parts in reality, I am convinced that my competence would secure applause. The point at which I stick, however, is this: rich men rarely do these things. It is the pursuit of wealth, rather than wealth itself, that is their pleasure. Let us suppose the case of a man who has toiled with undivided mind for thirty years to acquire a fortune; will it not be usually found that in the struggle to be rich he has lost those very qualities which make riches worth possessing? He buys his estate or builds his house; but there is little pleasure in the business. He is the mere slave of land-agents, the puppet of architects and upholsterers. He has no original taste to guide or interest him: what he once had has perished long ago in the dreary toil of money-grubbing. The men who build or decorate his house have a certain pleasure in their work; all that he does is to pay them for being happy. If he should adopt the rich man's hobby of collecting pictures or a library, he rarely enjoys a higher pleasure than the mere lust of possession. He buys what he is told to buy, without discrimination; he has no knowledge of what constitutes rarity or value; and most certainly he knows nothing of those excitements of the quest which make the collection of articles of vertu a pursuit so fascinating to the man of trained judgment but moderate means. And, as if to complete the irony of the situation, he is after all but the infrequent tenant of the treasure-house which he has built; the blinds are drawn half the year; the splendid rooms are seen by no wiser eyes than those of his butler and his housekeeper; and his secretary, if he be a man of taste and education, draws the real dividend of pleasure from all these rare and costly things which Dives has accumulated. Dives is in most cases little more than the man who pays the bill for things which other folk enjoy.

Let Dives be accounted then a public benefactor, we may say; perhaps so, but the question still remains, does Dives get the most and best out of life? The obvious answer is that the best things of life are not to be bought with money; it would be nearer the truth to quote the prophetic paradox, they are bought 'without money and without price.' I was present once at a dinner given by a millionaire newspaper proprietor to a crowd of journalists, on the occasion of the founding of a new magazine. The millionaire ate little, spoke little, and sat throughout the feast with an anxious cloud upon his brow. I recognised the same furtive look of apprehension in his eyes that I had seen in the eyes of my stock-broking friend long before. As I glanced round the room I found myself able to pick out all the men of wealth by that same look. It would seem that the anxieties of getting money only beget the more torturing anxiety of how to keep it. That, I am persuaded, was the dominant thought of my millionaire host throughout the meal; he knew the fear and fever of the gambler risking an enormous stake, the agitation of the soldier on the eve of a battle, in which victory is highly problematical. But that crowd of hungry journalists, how they did eat! What laughter sat on those boyish faces, what zest of life, what capacity of pleasure! There was not one of them whose daily bread was not precarious; not one perhaps who had a decent balance at the bank; yet they were so gay, so resolutely cheerful, so frankly interested in life and in themselves, that I could fancy those gloomy eyes at the head of the table watched them with a sort of envy, I think there must be something fatal to gaiety in the mere responsibilities of wealth; I am sure that there is something corrupting in the labours of its acquisition. I think I had rather be a vagrant, with a crust in my knapsack, a blue sky above me, and the adventurous road before me, than look upon the world with a pair of eyes so laughterless as his who was our host that night.

Again I protest that I make no railing accusation against wealth in itself. I am so far convinced of the truly beneficent utilities of wealth, that I would quite willingly take the risks of a moderate competence, should any one be disposed to make experiment with my virtues. There is some magnanimity in this offer, for I can no more foretell the effects of the bacillus of wealth upon my moral nature, than can the physician who offers his body for inoculation with the germ of some dire disease that science may be served. It argues some lack of imagination among millionaires that it has occurred to no one of the tribe to endow a man instead of an institution, if it were only by way of change. It would at least prove an interesting experiment, and it would be cheap at the price of the few unmissed thousands which the millionaire would pay for it. To such an experiment I would be willing to submit, if it were only to ascertain whether I have been right or wrong in my supposition that I am better qualified by nature than my fellows for the right administration of wealth; but there is one thing I would never do, I would never undertake that laborious quest of wealth, which robs men of the power to enjoy it when it is obtained.

It is there that the pinch comes; granted that some degree of competence is needed for a free and various use of life, is it worth while to destroy the power of living in attaining the means to live? What is a man better for his wealth if he does not know how to use it? A fool may steal a ship, but it takes a wise man to navigate her towards the islands of the Blest. I am told sometimes that there is a romance in business; no doubt there is, but it is pretty often the romance of piracy; and the pleasures of the rich man are very often nothing better than the pleasures of the pirate: a barbaric wading in gold, a reckless piling up of treasure, which he has not the sense to use. As long as there are shouting crews upon the sea and flaming ships, he is happy; but give him at last the gold which he has striven to win, and he knows nothing better than to sit like the successful pirate in a common ale-house, and make his boast to boon companions. I believe that the dullest men in all the world are very rich men; and I have sometimes thought that it cannot need a very high order of intelligence to acquire wealth, since some of the meanest of mankind appear to prosper at the business. A certain vulpine shrewdness of intelligence seems the thing most needed, and this may coexist with a general dulness of mind which would disgrace a savage.

The thing that is least perceived about wealth is that all pleasure in money ends at the point where economy becomes unnecessary. The man who can buy anything he covets, without any consultation with his banker, values nothing that he buys. There is a subtle pleasure in the extravagance that contests with prudence; in the anxious debates which we hold with ourselves whether we can or cannot afford a certain thing; in our attempts to justify our wisdom; in the risk and recklessness of our operations; in the long deferred and final joy of our possession; but this is a kind of pleasure which the man of boundless means never knows. The buying of pictures affords us an excellent illustration on this point. Men of the type of Balzac's *Cousin Pons* attain to rapture in the process because they are poor. They have to walk weary miles and wait long weeks to get upon the track of their treasure; to use all their knowledge of art and men to circumvent the malignity of dealers; to experience the extremes of trepidation and of hope; to deny themselves comforts, and perhaps food, that they may pay the price which has at last, after infinite dispute, reached an irreducible minimum; and the pleasure of their possession is in the ratio of their pains. But the man who enters a sale-room with the knowledge that he can have everything he wishes by the signing of a cheque feels none of these emotions. It seems to me that money has lost more than half its value since cheques became common. When men kept their gold in iron coffers, lock-fast cupboards, or a pot buried in an orchard, there was something tangible in wealth. When it came to counting out gold pieces in a bag, men remembered by what sweat of mind or body wealth was won, and they had a sense of parting with something which was really theirs. But a cheque has never yet impressed me with the least sense of its intrinsic value. It is a thing so trivial and fragile that the mind refuses to regard it as the equivalent of lands and houses and solid bullion. It is a thing incredible to reason that with a stroke of the pen a man may sign away his thousands. If cheques were prohibited by law, and all payments made in good coin of the realm, I believe we should all be much more careful in our expenditure, for we should have at least some true symbol of what expenditure implies.

In an ideal state all incomes beyond 10,000 pounds per year should be prohibited. Almost all the real luxuries of life may be enjoyed on half that sum; and even this is an excessive estimate. Such a regulation would be of vast advantage to the rich, simply because it would impose some limit at which economy commenced. They would then begin to enjoy their wealth. Avarice would decline, for obviously it would not be worth while to accumulate a larger fortune than the State permitted. We might also expect some improvement in manners, for there would be no room for that vulgar ostentation in which excessive wealth delights. If a man chose to exceed the limit which the law prescribed he would do so as a public benefactor; for, of course, the excess of wealth would be applied to the good of the community, in the relief of taxation, the adornment of cities, or the establishment of libraries and art-galleries. It would no doubt be objected that the great historic houses of the aristocracy could not be maintained on such an income; five thousand pounds a year would hardly pay the servants on a great estate, and provide the upkeep of a mansion. But in this case the State would become the custodian of such houses, which would be treated as national palaces. It is by no means improbable that their present owners would be glad to be rid of them on generous terms, which provided for a nominal ownership and an occasional occupation. However this may be, it is certain that the rich would profit by the change, for their chance of getting the most and best out of life would be much increased by the limit put upon cupidity and ostentation.

CHAPTER III

GETTING A LIVING, AND LIVING

Getting the best and most out of life, I take to be the most rational object of human existence. Even religion, although it affects to scorn the phrase, admits the fact; for no man would be religious unless he were convinced that he thereby added something to his store of happiness. It is a matter of temperament whether a man treats religion as a panacea for his mortal troubles, or the 'Open Sesame' of brighter worlds, but it is quite certain that he regards it as a means of happiness. I cannot doubt that the anchorites, ascetics, and cloistered nuns of mediaeval times were happy in their own way, although it was in a fashion that appears to us highly foolish and absurd. Even a St. Stylites had his consolations; he was kept warm upon his pillar by the comfortable sense of his superiority to his wicked fellow-creatures.

To get the best out of life there must be some adequate fulfilment of one's best self. Man is a bundle of tastes and appetites, some lofty, and some ignoble, but all crying out for satisfaction. Wisdom lies in the discernment of essentials; in just discrimination between false and true tastes. Man has been a long time upon the earth, and he has spent his time for the most part in one ceaseless experiment, viz., how he may become a satisfactory creature in his own eyes. All civilisations converge upon this point; and we maybe sure that, in their lonely hours of meditation, the fantastic warder on the great wall of China, and the Roman soldier pacing to and fro in the porticoes of the Palatine, had much the same thoughts. Whosoever speaks to man on the art of becoming happy is secure of a hearing; even though he be the vilest of quacks he will have his following, even though he were the worst of scoundrels some will take him for a prophet. In short, we are all the dupes of hope, and it needs some experience to assure us that our only real hope is in ourselves. In our own hearts lies the Eldorado which we scour the world to find; could we but fulfil our best selves we should ask no other happiness.

The question that soon comes to obtrude itself upon the mind of a thoughtful man in a great city, is this old persistent question of whether his method of life is such as to answer to the ideal of fulfilling his best self? It seemed to me that the inhabitants of cities were too busy getting a living to have time to live.

Let us take the life of the average business man by way of example. Such a man will rise early, sleep late, and eat the bread of carefulness, if he means to succeed. He will probably live—or be said to live—in some suburb more or less remote from the roaring centre of affairs. The first light of the winter dawn will see him alert; breakfast is a hurried passover performance; a certain train must be caught at all hazard to digestion, and the most leisured moments of the day will be those he passes in the railway carriage. Once arrived at his office he must plunge into the vortex of business; do battle with a thousand rivalries and competitions; day after day must labour in the same wearisome pursuits, content, perhaps, if at the end of the year he shall have escaped as by a miracle commercial shipwreck. He will come back to his residence, night after night, a tired man; not pleasantly wearied with pursuits which have exercised his complete powers, but tired to the point of dejection by the narrowness and monotony of his pursuits. I say he returns to his residence; I scorn to say his home, for the house he rents is merely the barrack where he sleeps. Of the life that goes on within this house, which is nominally his, he knows nothing. In its daily ordering, or even in its external features, he has no part. He has chosen no item of its furniture; he has had no hand in its decoration; he has but paid the tradesmen's bills. His children scarcely know him; they are asleep when he goes off in the morning, and asleep when he returns at night; he is to them the strange man who sits at the head of the table once a week and carves the Sunday joint. It is well for them if they have a mother who possesses gifts of government, sympathy, and patient comprehension, for it is clear that they have no father. He gets a living, and perhaps in time an ample living; but does he live?

It may be said that this picture is exaggerated; on the contrary, I think it is under-estimated. I have myself known men whose average daily absence from 'home' is twelve hours; they disappear by the eight o'clock morning train, and in times of special business pressure it is not far from midnight when they return. The trains, cabs, and public vehicles of London convey, day by day, one million three hundred thousand of these homeless men to their employments in the city. Here and there a wise man may be found who resents this tyranny of suburbanism. I know a young business man, who also chances to possess domestic instincts, for whom suburbanism grew so intolerable that he took a house in the very heart of London, that he might lunch and dine with his wife at his own table without neglecting his business interests. He was a wise man, but he is the only one I know. Counting the time passed at luncheon and dinner, the later departure in the morning, and the earlier arrival at night, he is the clear gainer, day by day, of three to four hours of domestic intercourse. At the end of the week he has thus added to the credit of his family life four-and-twenty hours; at the end of a year he has enjoyed more than fifty full days of domestic intercourse which would have been forfeited had he continued to live at Surbiton. He has also saved money, for though the rent he pays in Central London is more than the rent he paid at Surbiton, yet he has saved the expense of his season-ticket, lunches, and occasional dinners at a club or restaurant, and cabs to Waterloo when he was pressed for time. But it is quite vain to urge such considerations on the average man of business. He would tell you frankly that nothing would induce him to live in a house within a stone's-throw of Leicester Square, although it is a far better built and more comfortable house than the gimcrack villa which he rents at Surbiton. The gain in domestic intercourse would not attract him, for he has long ago lost taste for it; and the privilege of lunching with his family would repel him, for he is deeply suspicious of the virtues of domestic cookery. Nor, I suppose, would it influence him to tell him that by living in Central London, he could command without inconvenience the full attractions of the town, such as concerts, lectures, theatres, or those special assemblies which are representative of London life; for he desires nothing of the kind. Considerations of economy might affect him, but with all his skill at figures he seldom has the sense to see that the moiety of income paid yearly to the railway, by himself and his family, goes a long way toward the doubling of his rent. In short, suburbanism is his fetish; it is the keynote of his poor respectability, and he is not to be diverted from it by any reasons which a sane man would regard as considerable, if not imperative.

The most usual excuse of suburbanism is that it is a good thing for the wife and family of a business man, though it is a bad thing for him. It is singular that no one seems to recognise the gross selfishness of this plea. It is like the plea of the vivisectionist, that vivisection is a bad thing for a rabbit, but a very good thing for humanity, since humanity profits by the torture of the rabbit. But for my part I doubt whether there is any real profit to anybody in suburbanism. There is a town life, and there is a country life, each of which has peculiar compensations of its own; but suburbanism is a miserable compromise, which like most compromises combines not the qualities but the defects of two antagonisms. Its worst effect is that it sets up in one family two standards of life, which have nothing in common. After a while it must happen that there is a serious estrangement of taste, and it is not surprising if this often leads to a much more serious estrangement of affection. The air of Surbiton may be a little fresher than the air of Bloomsbury, but what does this count for if the atmosphere of the hearth be poisoned? Moreover, among the Anglo-Saxon peoples women are not encouraged to take any vital interest in the pursuits of their husbands as they are among the Latin races. I should not be surprised to find that half the women in the London suburbs do not know the precise nature of their husbands' occupations. A French woman of the bourgeois class often has a real aptitude for business. She can manage a shop, keep accounts, take an interest in markets, and in all questions of commercial enterprise she is the confidante, and often the adviser, of her husband. Your English woman of the same class prides herself rather on her total ignorance of business. It is probable that in twenty years of married life she has not once visited the warehouse or the office where her husband earns the income which she spends. She is 'provided for without the sweet sense of providing.' She sees her husband elated or depressed by things that have happened in the city; but to her the reasons of his hope or fear are not communicated, nor would she understand them if they were. His mind speaks a language foreign to her; his daily operations in the city have for her only the remote interest of things that have happened in a foreign country, which appear too unreal to excite any sincere sympathy or apprehension. Is this divided life good for either party?

Were some curious observer from another planet to arrive in London, I think few things would appear to him so extraordinary as a London suburb at noonday. By ten o'clock in the morning at latest he would see it denuded of all its male inhabitants. Like that fabulous realm of Tennyson's *Princess*, it is a realm inhabited by women; and the only male voice left in the land is the voice of the milk-boy on his rounds, the necessary postman, and the innocuous grocer's tout. There is something of the 'hushed seraglio' in these miles of trim houses, from whose doors and windows only female faces look out. An air of sensible bereavement lies upon the land. Woman, deprived of her lord and natural complement, cuts but a poor figure anywhere, but nowhere so poor as in a wide realm populous with grass widows. By what interests or avocations, or by what delinquency of duty the tedious hours are cheated, is not revealed to any male philosopher; but he is a poor observer who does not recognise something unnatural in this one-sided life. A few miles away the loud Niagara of London runs swift, and the air vibrates with all the tumult of the strenuous life of man; but here the air is dead, unwinnowed by any clamorous wind, unshaken by any planetary motion. I cannot think this narrow separated life good for woman, and I am surprised that in these days when woman claims equal privilege with man, she will submit to it. In the act of getting a living she also suffers, and loses something of the power to live. If the distraction of the city hurts the man she is not less injured by the torpor of the suburb. Let a woman be never so intelligent and keenly wrought, a suburb will soon enfeeble her, and take the fine edge off her spirit. Left to the sole society of nursemaids and cooks in her own house for many hours a day; to the companionship of women outside her house, whose conversation is mainly gossip about household difficulties; to the tame diversions of shopping at the nearest emporium; what power of interest in the larger things of life can be expected of her? The suburb is her cloister, and she the dedicated bride of littleness.

This seems a hard saying, but it can easily be verified by observation. I have myself known women, rich enough to keep a carriage, who had never been so far as Hyde Park, never visited the National Gallery, and never sought any finer music than could be furnished by a local concert. For them, London as an entity did not exist. This parochialism of suburban life is its most surprising feature. There is after all some excuse for Mr. Grant Allen's description of London as an aggregation of villages, when we find that so vast a number of Londoners really live the life of villagers. But it is not patriotism that binds them to the soil, nor local pride, as is the case with genuine villagers; it is rather sheer inertia. Such pride, if it existed, might do much for the regeneration of great cities, by creating a series of eager and intelligent communities, which would vie with one another in civic self-improvement; but this is just the kind of pride which does not exist. No one cares how his suburb is misgoverned, so long as rates are not too exorbitant. A suburb will wake into momentary life to curb the liberal programmes of the school-board, or to vote against the establishment of a free library; a gross self-interest being thus the only variation of its apathy. It soon falls asleep again, dulled into torpor by the fumes of its own intolerant smugness. For much of this the element of family separation in suburban life is answerable. The men pay their rates and house-rent at Surbiton, but they live their real lives within hearing of the bell of St. Paul's; how should they take any interest in Surbiton? After all, Surbiton is to them but a vast caravansary, where they are lodged and fed at night; and one does not inquire too closely into the internal amenities of his hotel so long as the food is tolerable, and the bed clean.

Suburbanism is, however, but a branch, though an important branch, of the larger question, whether in cities men do not ultimately sacrifice the finer qualities and joys of life to the act of getting a living. It will perhaps be said that the man with a true genius for business must in any case live in a city; that he is not discontented with the conditions of his life; that, all things being considered, he is probably living the kind of life for which he is best fitted. May not a writer, who is presumably a person of studious and quiet habits, misinterpret the life of a business man precisely in the same way that he misinterprets the life of the poor, by applying to it his own standards instead of measuring it by theirs? Business, for the man of business genius, is more than an employment; it is his epic, his romance, his adventurous crusade. He brings to it something of the statesman's prescience, the diplomatist's sagacity, the great captain's power of organising victory. His days are battles, his life a long campaign; and if he does not win the spoil of kingdoms, he does fight for commercial supremacy, which comes to much the same thing. No doubt there is much truth in this putting of the case, though it really begs the main question. But even if we grant that in the larger operations of commerce a certain type of genius is required, we must remember that the men of this order are few in number. Every lord of commerce is attended by a vast retinue of slaves. Very few of these humble servitors of commerce can ever hope to rise from the ranks into supreme command. They must labour to create the wealth of the successful merchant as a private soldier suffers wounds and hardships that fame may crown his general. Do these men share the higher privileges of life? Is not life with them the getting of a living rather than living? Nay, more; is it not the getting of a living for some one else?

The merchant-prince fulfils himself, for his highest powers of intelligence are daily taxed to the uttermost; but the case is very different with that vast army of subordinates, whom we see marching every morning in an infinite procession to the various warehouses and offices of London. I have often wondered at their cheerfulness when I have recollected the nature of their life. For they bring to their daily tasks not the whole of themselves, but a mere segment of themselves; some small industrious faculty which represents them, or misrepresents them, at the tribunal of those who ask no better thing of them. Few of them are doing the best that they can do, and they know it. They are not doing it because the world does not ask them to do it; indeed, the world takes care that they shall have no opportunity of doing it. A certain faculty for arithmetic represents a man who has many higher faculties; and thus the man is forced to live by one capacity which is perhaps his least worthy and significant. This is not the case in what we call the liberal professions and the arts. The architect, the barrister, the humblest journalist needs his whole mind for his task, and hence his work is a delight. The artist, if he be a true artist, does the one thing that he was born to do, and so 'the hours pass away untold, without chagrin, and without weariness,' nor would he wish them to pass otherwise. Many times as I took my way to the dreary labours of my desk I stopped to watch, and sometimes to talk with, a smiling industrious little Frenchman, who repaired china and bronzes in a dingy shop in Welbeck Street. He was an expert at his trade; knew all the distinctive marks of old china, and could assign with certainty the right date of any piece of bronze he handled; and to hear him discourse on these things would have been a liberal education to a budding connoisseur. I never knew a man so indefatigably happy in his work; his eye lit up at any special glow of colour or delicacy of design; he used his tools as though he loved them; and if he dreamed at night, I doubt not that his canopies were coloured with the hues of Sèvres, and that bronze angels from the hand of Benvenuto stood about his bed. Plainly the man was happy because his work engaged his whole attention; and to every cunning rivet that he fashioned he gave the entire forces of his mind. Here was a man who not merely got a living but lived; and I, chained to my desk, knew well enough that his life was much more satisfactory than mine.

Money has little to do with this problem of satisfactory living; I think that this was the first discovery I made in the direction of a better mode of life. My French workman earned perhaps two pounds a week: I earned four or five; but he bought happiness with his work, whereas I bought discontent and weariness. Money may be bought at too dear a rate. The average citizen, if he did but know it, is always buying money too dear. He earns, let us say, four hundred pounds a year; but the larger proportion of this sum goes in what is called 'keeping up appearances.' He must live in a house at a certain rental; by the time that his rates and taxes are paid he finds one-eighth of his income at least has gone to provide a shelter for his head. A cottage, at ten pounds a year, would have served him better, and would have been equally commodious. He must needs send his children to some private 'academy' for education, getting only bad education and high charges for his pains; a village board-school at twopence a week would have offered undeniable advantages. He must wear the black coat and top-hat sacred to the clerking tribe; a tweed suit and cap are more comfortable, and half the price. At all points he is the slave of convention, and he pays a price for his convention out of all proportion to its value. At a moderate estimate half the daily expenditure of London is a sacrifice to the convention or imposture of respectability.

Unless a man have, however, a large endowment of that liberal discontent which makes him perpetually examine and reexamine the conditions of his life, he will be a long time before he even suspects that he is the victim of artificial needs. When once the yoke of habit is imposed, the shoulder soon accustoms itself to the bondage, and the aches and bruises of initiation are forgotten. There are spasms of disgust, moments of wise suspicion; but they are transient, and men soon come to regard a city as the prison from whence there is no escape. But is no escape possible? That was the question which pressed more and more upon me as the years went on. I saw that the crux of the whole problem was economic, I knew that I was not the gainer by a larger income, if I could buy a more real satisfaction on less income. I saw that it was the artificial needs of life that made me a slave; the real needs of life were few. A cottage and a hundred pounds a year in a village meant happiness and independence; but dared I sacrifice twice or thrice the income to secure it? The debate went on for years, and it was ended only when I applied to it one fixed and reasoned principle. That principle was that my first business as a rational creature was *not to get a living but to live*; and that I was a fool to sacrifice the power of living in securing the means of life.

CHAPTER IV

EARTH-HUNGER

Like Charles II., who apologised for being so unconscionably long in dying, I must apologise for being so long in coming to my point, which is the possibility of buying happiness at a cheaper rate than London offers it. As it took me twenty years of experience to make my discovery, I may claim, however, that three chapters is no immoderate amount of matter in which to describe it. My chief occupation through these years was to keep my discontent alive. Satisfaction is the death of progress, and I knew well that if I once acquiesced entirely in the conditions of my life, my fate was sealed.

I did not acquiesce, though the temper of my revolt was by no means steady. There were times when—to reverse an ancient saying—the muddy Jordan of London life seemed more to me than all the sparkling waters of Damascus. Humanity seemed indescribably majestic; and there were moments when I sincerely felt that I would not exchange the trampled causeways of the London streets for the greenest meadows that bordered Rotha or Derwentwater. There were days of early summer when London rose from her morning bath of mist in a splendour truly unapproachable; when no music heard of man seemed comparable with the long diapason of the crowded streets; when from morn to eve the hours ran with an inconceivable gaiety and lightness, and the eye was in turn inebriated with the hard glare and deep shadows of abundant light, with the infinite contrasts of the streets, with the far-ranged dignity of domes and towers swimming in the golden haze of midday, or melting in the lilac mists of evening. I felt also, in this vast congregation of my fellow-creatures, the exhilarating sense of my own insignificance. Of what value were my own opinions, hopes, or programmes in this huge concourse and confusion of opinion? Who cared what one human brain chanced to think, where so many million brains were thinking? I was swept on like a bubble in the stream, and I forgot my own individuality. And this forgetfulness became a pleasure; the mind, wearied of its own affairs, found delight in recollecting that the things that seemed so great to it were after all of infinitesimal importance in the general sum of things.

Astronomy is often credited with providing this sensation; writers of fiction especially are fond of explaining how the voyage of the eye through space humbles the individual pride of man through the oppression of magnitude and vastness. They might come nearer home, for terrestrial magnitudes produce the same effect as celestial magnitudes; the mind loses itself as readily in the abyss of London as in those gulfs of chaos that open in the Milky Way, confronting the eye with naked infinitude; and this sense of personal insignificance is at once a horror and a joy. That humble acquiescence of the Londoner in his fate which we call his apathy, is the natural consequence of an overwhelming sense of personal insignificance. The great reformer should be country-born; in the solitude of nature he may come to think himself significant, and have faith in those thoughts and intuitions which no one contradicts. But in London, collective life, by its mere immensity, overwhelms individual life so completely that no audacity or arrogance of genius can supply that continuous and firm faith in himself which the reformer must possess.

If I resisted these debilitating influences, it was through no particular virtue of my own: it was rather through what I may call a kind of earth-hunger. I had an obstinate craving for fresh air, unimpeded movement, outdoor life. I wanted the earth, and I wanted to live in the close embrace of the earth. Some ancestor of mine must have been a hermit on a mountain, a gipsy, or a peasant: I know not which, but something of the temperament of all three had been bequeathed to me. The smell of fresh-turned earth was a smell that revived in me a portion of my nature that had seemed dead; a flower set me dreaming of solitary woods; and I found myself watching clouds and weather-signs as though my bread depended on their lenience. The first time I saw a mountain I burst into tears, an act which astonished me no less than my companions. I could offer no explanation of my conduct, but I felt as though the mountain called me. I said to myself, 'There is my home, yonder is the earth of which my corporeal part is fashioned; it is there that I should live and die.' Even a London park in the first freshness of a summer morning produced these sensations; and those rare excursions which I took into the genuine country left me aching for days afterwards with an exquisite pain. I often imagined myself living as Wordsworth did in Dove Cottage, as Thoreau did in the Walden Woods, and the vision was delightful. I took an agricultural paper, and read it diligently, not because it was of the least practical utility to me, but because its simple details of country life seemed to me a kind of poetry. In my rambles I never saw a lovely site without at once going to work to build an imaginary cottage on it, and the views I had from the windows of my dream-cottages were more real to me than the actual prospects on which I looked every day. I have even gone so far as to seek the offices of land-agents, and haggle over the price of land which I never meant to buy, for the mere pleasure of fancying it was mine; and this kind of game was long pursued, for land-agents are a numerous tribe, and when one discovered my imposture, there was always another ready to accept me as a capitalist in search of the picturesque. In short, to possess one small fragment of the world's surface; to have a hut, a cabin, or a cottage that was verily my own, to eat the fruits of my own labour on the soil—this seemed to me the crown and goal of all human felicity. Conscript of the city as I was, drilled and driven daily in the grim barrack-yard of despotic civilisation, yet I was a deserter at heart; an earth-hunger as rapacious and intense as that of any French or Irish peasant burned in my bones, and, like the peasant conscript that I truly was, my dreams were all of green pastures and running streams, and the happy loneliness of open spaces under open skies.

This kind of earth-hunger is, I believe, not common among English people to-day; if it were, the tide of life would not set so steadily townward as it does. The class in which it existed most strongly was the yeoman class, and this is a class which has practically disappeared. In my youth I knew half a dozen persons of this class, to whom towns were genuinely abhorrent. They would come to London once or twice in their lives, visit certain market towns in their district at intervals, and escape back into the country with the joy of wild birds liberated from a cage. The mere grime and dirt of cities horrified them; they were suffocated in the close air, and they were driven half distracted by the clamour of the streets. These men lived, upon the whole, lives of not immoderate labour: or, as one might say, of sober ease, They possessed little money, it is true, but the want of it did not appear to trouble them. Their houses were plain, their method of life simple, and clearly it had not entered their minds to covet any more sumptuous modes of life. All this is changed now. The daily press, which presents a thousand pictures of the bustling life of cities, goes everywhere, and has communicated a strange restlessness to the rural mind. Increased means of locomotion have brought London to the very door of village communities. If men to-day actually possessed the acres on which they toil they would be in no hurry to leave them; they would be effectually chained to the soil by the sense of independence and proprietorship, as is the case among the rural population of France, who do not rent but own the land. The yeomen did own the land, and that was the secret of their content. But when the day of large farms came, the small landowners were crushed out; and as for the mere peasant, he has no chance at all of ever owning land, and never has had; so that he has every inducement to crowd into towns where wages are nominally higher, and he soon outgrows that natural earth-hunger which modern civilisation affords him no means of gratifying.

By virtue of the peasant or gipsy blood in me I kept my earth-hunger through twenty years of London life, but I count my case unique. I never found any one who shared my feelings; on the contrary, I found that whatever primitive instincts toward country life my friends may have had once, London had made an effectual end of them. The country means for most Londoners, not the blessed solitude of open spaces, but Margate or Brighton. When the annual summer exodus arrives he does but exchange one kind of town for another kind. He carries with him all the aptitudes and artificial instincts of the town; he loves the bustle of a crowd; he wants boarding-houses full of company, and streets brilliant with electric light; and he returns to town, after a vivacious fortnight, without having once looked upon the real country, unless it be with the distracted eye of a rider on a *char-à-banc*. If my earth-hunger did not die in London, it was mainly because my holidays were of a very different description. I never visited but one watering-place, and that was enough. I never stayed in a boarding-house in my life, nor would the promise of all my expenses paid and a handsome bonus into the bargain tempt me to the experiment. I sought the country absolute; a cottage or a little farm remote from towns and out of sound of railways; villages so tiny that maps refuse to name them. I can count half a dozen of these places which haunt my memory with all the sanctity of some religious dream. They were my temporary cloisters, where

When I lived among these simple folk I shared not only their roof but their labours, and it was thus I came to distinguish between the nature of work in cities and work in the country. To obtain my meal in a city I had to do things that were distasteful to me; I had to shut myself away from the fresh air and sunlight in a dingy room and to spend dull hours in tasks which afforded me no genuine intellectual pleasure. Here, on the contrary, every duty had a pastime yoked with it. I rose early, not only that I might learn to milk the cows, but that I might see the sunrise; if I went into the woods to saw logs that would presently make a clear flame on the evening fire, my lungs drank health among the forest fragrances; when I went fishing I did something not only pleasurable but useful, for I added dainties to my larder. In the city I lived to work; here I worked to live. I might go further and say that in the city I lived to work for other people, for my brains were daily exploited that my master might maintain a house at Kensington, and when the landlord, the water-lord, the light-lord, and the rate-collector had all had their dues from me there was little enough left that I could call my own. Here, on the contrary, all that I did had an immediate and direct relation to my own well-being. The amount of work I had to do to live was light, and I bought with it something that was my own. We are so used to the exactions of a complicated and artificial life, that it is an amazing discovery to ascertain how small is the toll of labour which Nature asks of those who live naturally. You have but to do certain things which in themselves are pleasures to obtain ample means of life; and as these things are soon and easily done by a healthy human creature there is an abundant leisure at his command. To split pine-logs, dig a garden, pull a heavy boat down the lake after fish, tramp up the hillside to collect the sheep, are simply so many exercises of the body, the equivalents of which town youths find in the gymnasium or the football field; the difference is that all this exertion in the gymnasium, which the town youth takes to keep up his health, would in the country *keep him.* The same amount of muscular exertion which a town youth puts forth to chase a ball round a twenty acre field would, if properly applied, put a roof over his head and food on his table. The sports of the civilised man are means of life to the natural man. If a man must needs sweat, and be bemired, and have an aching back, it is surely better economy to have a house and a good meal at the end of it all than merely a good appetite for a meal that he has yet to pay for. I do not object to buy health in hard physical exercise if I can buy it in no other way; but I am better satisfied if I can buy health and a meal at the same time and for the same price. This is practically what is done every day by men who live in the country. In a town they would undertake an equal amount of muscular exertion for the sake of health, and would find that they still had 'to go to business' to live; here they have done their business in doing their pleasure.

Earth-hunger is without doubt the most wholesome passion men can entertain, and if Governments were wise they would do all they could to fortify and gratify it. On the contrary, the settled policy of English Government is entirely hostile to it. There is no country where it is so difficult to acquire freehold land in small quantities—a subject on which I shall have more to say presently. Bad land-laws lie at the back of what we call the urban tendencies of modern life. If fifty years ago the Irish peasantry had had the same facilities for acquiring land that they have to-day, it is safe to say that there would have been little or no emigration, for never was there race that left the land of its fathers with such bitter and entire reluctance as the Irish. The English peasant shares the same reluctance, though his slower nature is incapable of expressing it with the same volubility of anguish. Give him enough land to live upon; make him a proprietor instead of a serf; let him have fair railway rates, so that his produce can fetch its proper price in the markets, and there were no man so proud and so content as he. But this is just what the feudal laws of England will not do for him; and so millions of acres fall out of cultivation and farms go a-begging because the men who could have kept them prosperous have been forced to sell their thews and muscles to be prostituted in the dismal drudgeries of cities.

There is an even worse result. Earth-hunger has been displaced by Money-hunger. Simple ideas of life must needs perish where the nature of a nation's life makes them difficult or impossible of attainment. A country-born youth might keep to the soil, if he saw the slightest hope that the soil would keep him; when he sees that this is impossible he files to cities, because he believes that there is more gold to be picked up in the city mire in a month than can be won from the ploughed fallow in a year. It is not until the altars of Pan are overthrown that the worship of Mammon is triumphant, and the mischief is that when the great god Pan is driven away he returns no more. When once Money-hunger seizes on a nation, that primitive and wholesome Earth-hunger—old as the primal Eden, where man's life began—is stifled at the birth; the spade and harrow rust, and instead of swords being beaten to ploughshares, ploughshares are beaten into swords for the use of soldiers who are the gladiators of commercial avarice; the wealth of the country runs into the swamp of speculation; the scripture of Nature is cast aside for the blotted pages of the betting-book; sport becomes not a means of recreation but of gambling; and instead of sturdy races bred upon the soil, and drawing from the soil solid qualities of mind and body, you have blighted and anaemic races, bred amid the populous disease of cities, and incapable of any task that shall demand steady energy, continuous thought, or sober powers of reflection or of will.

CHAPTER V

HEALTH AND ECONOMICS

Enough has been said to show that I never heartily settled to a town life, and that the obstacle to content was my own character. Mere discontent with one's environment, however useful it may be as an irritant to prevent stagnation and brutish acquiescence, obviously does not carry one very far. Men may chafe for years at the conditions of their lot without in any way attempting to amend them. I soon came to see that I was in danger of falling into this condition of futility. I was, therefore, forced to face the question whether my continual inward protest against the kind of life which I led was founded on anything more stable than an opinion or a sentiment? No man ever yet took a positively heroic or original course for the sake of an opinion. Opinion must become conviction before it has any potency to change the ordering of life. I saw plainly that I must either bring my thoughts to the point of conviction or discard them altogether.

There is a good phrase which is sometimes used about men who are members of a party, without in any way entering into its propagandist aims—we say that they 'do not play the game.' They may have excellent philosophic reasons for their aloofness, or even admirable scruples; but parties do not ask for either. Parties ask for party loyalty, and to give this loyalty personal scruples must be set aside. I could not but apply this doctrine to my own state of mind. London asked me to play the game, and I was not playing it. It was impossible to put heart into a kind of life which I inwardly detested. I did my day's work with a mind divided; and, although no one could accuse me of wilful negligence, yet a child could see that my work missed that quality of entire efficiency which makes for success. I might count myself much superior to men like Arrowsmith by the possession of superior sentiments, yet, in the long run, my sentiment debilitated me, and his destitution of sentiment was a source of power to him in the kind of work we both had to do. To the man who detests the nature of his employment as I detested mine, I would say at once, either conquer your detestation or change your work. Work that is not genuinely loved cannot possibly be done well. It is no use chafing and fretting and wishing that you lived in the country, if you know perfectly well that you have not the least intention of living anywhere but in the town. If it is town life you are really bent upon, the sooner rustic instincts are uprooted the better for you. London can prove herself a complaisant mistress to those who desire no other, but she will give nothing to those who flout her in their hearts. In plain words there is no middle course between accepting the yoke or finally rejecting it; either course may be justified, but it is the silliest folly to accept with complacency a yoke which you mean to shake off the moment you have courage or opportunity to revolt. London marks such dissemblers with an angry eye, as captains mark reluctant soldiers; and if time holds no disgrace for them it will certainly bring them no advancement.

Were my fine theories composed of mere fluid sentiment, or had they some more consistent element in them which was capable of hardening into invincible conviction? That was my problem. It was debated in season and out of season. Gradually the two dominant factors in the problem became evident; they were health and economics.

There could be no question about health. It was true that I had suffered from no serious illness in my life, but London kept me in a normal state of low vitality. I had constant headaches, fits of depression, and minor physical derangements. I rarely knew what it was to wake in the morning with that clear joyousness of spirit which marks vigorous vitality. A London winter I dreaded, and I had good reason for my dread. When the fog lay on the town an unbearable oppression lay also on my spirits. Imagination had little to do with this oppression; it was the physical result of lack of oxygen. It was the same with my children; they grew pinched and bleached in face, and went about their little tasks with the slowness of old men. It is stated, I believe, that London is the healthiest city in the world; no doubt it is true as regards the actual percentage of disease to the immense population, but statistics take no account of lowered vitality. Without being actually ill, vitality may be reduced to a point at which existence becomes a kind of misery. Alcohol dissolves for a time the cloud on the mind, the incubus upon the energies; and the relief is so great that men do not think of the price they pay for it. No wonder public-houses are the landmarks of London locomotion; they are the Temples of Oblivion, where the devitalised multitudes seek to forget themselves, that they may regain the courage to live at all.

For myself, I had sense to know that stimulants of this kind were a remedy much worse than the disease. The only stimulant, at once safe and effectual, which I needed was fresh air. The moment I found myself among the hills a miraculous change was wrought in me. I had not breathed that quick and vital air for an hour before a glow ran through my veins more delightful, and much more enduring, than the glow of wine. A single night in some small cottage chamber—where the very bed had a cool scent of flowers and lawns, where the open window admitted air fresh from pine forest and mountain streams, where the silence was so deep that one's pulse seemed to tick aloud like a watch—and I awoke a man renewed. Six o'clock, or even five, was not too soon for all my little household to be astir. We were all alike eager for the open air; for the walk, bare-footed, through the dewy grass to the mountain pool; for the shock and thrill of that green water into which we plunged delighted; and in those prolonged and pure ablutions I think our spirits shared. The bells of laughter rang the livelong day. The cramped mind began to move again, and long abdicated powers of fancy and of humour were restored. Equanimity of body brought evenness of temper; it was incredible to recollect how irritable we had been with one another in those ghastly days of London fog, when the very grating of a chair along the floor made the nerves jump. Even the mind took new edge, for though I did not read much upon a holiday, yet I found that what I did read left a clearness of impression to which I had long been unaccustomed. And what was the root and cause of all this miracle? Fresh air, wholesome food, rude health—nothing more! To feel that it is bliss to be alive, health alone is needed. And by health I mean not the absence of physical ailment or disease, but a high condition of vitality. This the country gave me; this the town denied me. The only question was then, at what rate did I value the boon?

This brought me immediately to the much more complex problem of economics. I knew that men could live in the country on small means, for men did so; but I perceived that the art of living in the country did not come by nature. Every one supposes that he can drive a horse or grow potatoes; and, when we recollect how many thousands of men go to Canada to take up agricultural pursuits without the least knowledge of the business, it is clear that the belief is general that any man can farm. I may claim the merit of freedom from this popular delusion. I not only knew that I could not farm, but I did not wish to be a farmer. What I wished was to live in the country in some modest way that answered to my needs; to earn by some form of exertion a small income; and at the most, to grow my own vegetables, catch my own fish, and snare my own rabbits.

A legacy of two hundred a year would have served my purpose admirably, but modesty forbade me laying my case before benevolent millionaires, and a destitution of maiden aunts put an end to any hopes of a bequest by natural causes.

What was my precise position then? I had a salary of two hundred and fifty pounds a year. An investment that had turned out fortunately gave me about forty pounds a year. I had done from time to time a little work for the press, which had been worth to me about thirty pounds a year more. My total budget showed, then, an annual income of three hundred and twenty pounds, which I found barely sufficient for my needs as a dweller in towns. If I migrated to a cottage, how would matters stand with me? I should lose my two hundred and fifty pounds per annum of course, and this was an alarming prospect. But, on the other hand, I reminded myself that I had never really possessed it. I prepared various tables in which I arranged the items of my expenditure under two heads, viz. the expenditure that was inevitable, and the expenditure that was evitable, because it was the result of town life. I shall best explain by giving a sample of these tables:—

TABLE I.

INEVITABLE EXPENDITURE. L. s. d.

    Food and general household expenses,
  calculated at 30s. per week 78 0 0
 Books, magazines, and papers 5 0 0
 Clothes for two adults and two children . 20 0 0
 Insurances 25 0 0
 Holidays 30 0 0
 Education 35 0 0
 Sundries 10 0 0

Rent, rates, and taxes 65 0 0
_____
L268 0 0

TABLE II.

EVITABLE EXPENDITURE.

If I adopted a country life. L. s. d.

Holidays 30 0 0
By saving on rent, rates, and taxes,
  calculating my cottage cost me not
  more than L20 per annum 45 0 0
By saving in food 20 0 0
_____
L95 0 0

It will be seen that I allowed no reduction in clothes and books, for I did not wish my children to be dressed as beggars, or to be ignorant of current literature.

It does not need the eye of a chartered accountant to perceive that whatever may be said for Table II., Table I. is not satisfactory. In it I accounted for only 268 pounds, whereas I have already stated my total income was 320 pounds. What became of the 52 pounds which found no record in my ingenuous schedule? I could not tell, but I was pretty sure that it was absorbed in the petty wastefulness of town life. Londoners are so accustomed to constant daily expenditure in small ways, that it occurs to no one to ascertain how considerable an encroachment this aggregate expenditure is upon the total yearly income. In all but very fine weather I must needs use some means of public conveyance every day; there was a daily lunch to be provided; and when work kept me late at the office there was tea as well. One can lunch comfortably on a shilling or eighteenpence a day; and I knew places where I could have lunched for much less, but they were in parts of the town which I could not reach in the brief time at my disposal. Moreover, one must needs be the slave of etiquette even though he be a clerk, and if all the staff of an office frequent a certain restaurant, one must perforce fall into line with them under penalty of social ostracism. Thus, whether I liked it or not, for five days in the week I had to spend eighteenpence a day for lunch, and fourpence for teas; and if we add those small gratuities which the poorest men take it as a point of honour to observe, here was an annual expenditure of 25 pounds. Taking one thing with another 5 pounds might be added for 'bus and railway fares; so that only 22 pounds is left to be accounted for. And now, if we return to Table II., it is obvious that my income of 320 pounds per annum was only nominal, because a very great part of it was really spent in keeping up a position which a town life imposed upon me. Before I touched a single penny of my nominal income of 250 pounds per annum, I had paid 30 pounds per year in the daily expenses inevitable to my position, and 65 pounds for rent and taxes, which was quite 45 pounds more than I ought to pay. Education comes also to be considered at this point. My two children went to a very respectable school at the cost of a little more than 15 pounds per annum each. No doubt I might have sent them to a Board school, where they would have received a better education; but in the part of London where I lived there was no Board school within easy reach, and besides this, though I hate the pretension of gentility, manners and companionship have to be considered as well as education in the choice of a school. A child may take no harm by sitting on the same bench with village children, but the London gamin is not a desirable acquaintance. In this, as in other matters, I paid through the nose for my position; and the convention cost me a clear 35 pounds per annum. Thus I calculated that out of a nominal income of

250 pounds per annum 100 pounds was paid as a tax to convention and respectability.

I have no doubt that a good many flaws may be found in these calculations; but one point is beyond dispute, viz., that a town income is always more apparent than real. Money is worth no more than its purchasing power. The business man who is offered 1000 pounds per annum in New York against 700 pounds per annum in London, refuses the offer unless it carries with it great contingent advantages, because he knows perfectly well that 700 pounds a year in London is worth a good deal more than 1000 pounds a year in New York. But the same kind of prudent calculation is seldom applied to the case of town versus country living at home. It is impossible to persuade the labourer that a pound a week in London is really less than fifteen shillings a week in the country. Men are dazzled by mere figures, and there is no country clerk who would not jump at the idea of a fifty pounds a year rise in London, though ten minutes spent over a sum in addition and subtraction would be sufficient to assure him that he would not be enlarging his income but diminishing it. A man has to live upon a certain scale suited to his needs and tastes, but the income which makes this kind of life possible is a variable quantity. It is not by what men earn in the aggregate that their incomes should be measured, but by what they have left when the necessary cost of living is defrayed. If it costs a man fifty pounds a year more to live in London than in the country, he is obviously no better off by the extra fifty pounds he earns in London. He is not earning fifty pounds for himself but fifty pounds for the landlord, the rate-collector, the gas-man, the restaurant proprietor, the omnibus and railway companies. His gold never reaches his own pocket; it is filched from him by dexterous thieves; it gleams before him for an instant like the coin spun in the air by the conjurer or thimble-rigger, and then vanishes for ever. Yet I have found few men keen enough to penetrate the delusion; it would seem they love to be deluded, and by their conduct justify the satiric lines of *Hudibras*—

> Doubtless the pleasure is as great
> To cheated be as 'tis to cheat.

In most things I claim to be no wiser than my fellow-men, but in this I knew myself wiser; I knew where I was cheated. I knew that the schoolmaster who cost me thirty pounds a year was a licensed footpad; half the money spent in restaurants and tea-shops was blackmail paid to respectability; the landlord who took his forty-five pounds a year from my pocket was a mere robber, who took advantage of the need I had to live in a certain locality that I might attend to my vocation. Not only were my brains exploited that my employer might maintain a sumptuous house at Kensington, but the wage he paid me was exploited by a host of other people, who had houses of their own to maintain. Before I could feed my children I must help to pay for and cook the dinner of the folk who lived on the dividends of railways and omnibus companies. On the way to my office the tailor took toll of me by forcing me to wear a garb which I detested, simply because I dared wear no other garb. I could not even drink plain water but that some one was the richer. I was the common gull of the thing called convention. I was plucked to the skin, and if my skin had been worth turning into leather, some one would have put in a claim to that. Even for my skin, poor asset as it was, some one did wait, when it had ceased to be of use to me, for London cemeteries declare dividends upon the dead. My case reminded me of an old gentleman I once knew, who wore so many coats, waistcoats, and shirts to keep warmth in a body of singular attenuation, that it was commonly said that by the time James Smith undressed at night there was very little James Smith that was discoverable. Certainly by the time London had done wringing gold out of me there was very little gold left that was my own.

There was, however, one kind of comfort to be deduced from these reflections; if I was not nearly so well off as I appeared to be, I had all the less to lose. Rightly considered it would not be 250 pounds per annum that I should lose by leaving London, for I had never possessed that sum, I calculated my real loss at something nearer 150 pounds, and this seemed not so terrible a thing. I had my forty pounds a year for certain. I had the small earnings of my pen, and with abundant time upon my hands I saw every reason why these should be increased. Could I face a new kind of life upon an income of seventy pounds per annum? Ah, how anxiously that problem was debated with my wife, many a night when the children were abed! The natural conservatism of woman had a great deal to say in these debates. 'It was all very well,' said my wife, 'to do these little sums on paper, but suppose the facts did not correspond? Suppose I found no cottage at twenty pounds a year, and no decent school at sixpence a week? Then the world was full of writers for the press.' (I frowned.) 'Not of course like you, not half so good,' she added with a smile, 'but how do you know that you will succeed? Show me a fixed income of 100 pounds a year, and I would chance it, for I can live simply enough,' she would say, 'and am as fond of liberty as you.'

She might have added what I knew to be true, that the penalties of London life fell heavier upon her than me. I was not insensible to the instantaneous lightening of spirits that happened with her when she was able to forsake the abominable purlieus of the cellar-kitchen where her life was spent; and although I knew not half her toils, nor half her dejections and anxieties, which were sedulously kept from me, yet I was not wholly blind. I had seen her too amid the roses of a cottage garden flying the colour of long-forgotten roses in her cheeks; in the hay-field shaking off a dozen years in as many hours; and although she was always young to me, she never seemed so young and sweet as when we walked a honeysuckled lane together. Her desire was with me I knew well; she had no fear of poverty, and would have been content with plainer fare than I; but her children made her prudent.

At last the one thing happened which made her prudence coincide with her desires; one of the children sickened with a languor that was the precursor of disease, and the doctors said that only country air could bring back strength. And then fate itself took the whole matter out of my control. Something happened in the city—I know not what—and the firm I served came near to shipwreck. Business shrank to a diminished channel, and the staff of clerks must needs be reduced. I have said some hard words of my employer as the exploiter of my labour; he will appear no more in this history, and my last word about him shall be justly kind. He broke the news of his misfortune to me with a delicacy that made me respect him, and with a hesitating painful shame that made me pity him. He praised me beyond my merit for my twenty years of service; he had hoped to keep me with him for another twenty years, and I believe he spoke the truth when he said it pained him to think that his misfortunes should be mine. He handed me in silence a cheque for fifty pounds. He then shook my hand heartily, murmured some vague words about hoping to reinstate me if things should mend, and hurried from me; and in his broken look and bowed shoulders I read the prophecy that his days of fortune and success were gone for ever. The little tragedy was played out in less than ten minutes. I locked my desk, put on my hat and coat, and went out into the street; and my heart felt a pang at leaving the place which I should never have imagined possible. I had walked fully half a mile before another thought occurred to me. My blood suddenly sang in my veins, and I remembered that I was an emancipated slave; at last I was Free!

CHAPTER VI

IN SEARCH OF THE PICTURESQUE

I was free, but what was I to do with my freedom? Ingenious apologists for slavery used to argue that the slave was much happier as a bondman than a freeman, as long as the conditions of his bondage were not unendurably harsh: but no one ever knew a slave who held this creed. There never was a slave who did not prefer his dinner of herbs, earned by his own labour, to the stalled ox of luxurious captivity. For my part, I thought the air never tasted so sweet as on that morning of my liberation. I walked slowly, drawing long breaths, that I might taste its full relish, as a connoisseur passes an exquisite and rare wine over his palate, that he may discriminate its subtleties. I became a lounger, and took the pavement with the air of a gentleman at ease. I wandered into Hyde Park, paid my penny for a seat, and sat down almost dizzy with the unaccustomed thought that there was not a human being in the universe who, at that moment, had the smallest claim to make upon my time or energy. An hour passed in a kind of ecstatic dream. It chanced to be a morning when Queen Victoria was driving from Paddington to Buckingham Palace, and every instant the throng of carriages increased. Standing on my seat, I saw an immense lane of people, silent as a wood; a contagious shiver stirred them, like a gust of wind amongst the leaves; I saw the distant glitter of helmets and cuirasses, and the pageant swept along with that one tired, kindly, homely face for its centre of attraction, luring loyalty even from a heart so republican as mine by its air of patient weariness. I thought, and I believed the thought sincere, that I would not have exchanged places with her who was the mistress of so many peoples, the Empress of such indeterminable Empire. My new-born loyalty was three-parts pity. Had she, who sat there in such 'lonely splendour,' ever known the day, since as a young girl the heavy rod of empire was intrusted to her frail and unaccustomed hands, when she woke to say, 'This day I am free, I will go where I will, do as I please, and none shall stay me?' Yet I, a manumitted clerk, had come upon this singular and glad day; and I had it in my heart to say with Emerson, 'Give me health and a day, and I will make the pomp of empire ridiculous.'

I turned slowly homeward in this glow of exultation. I should have run, for the news, either good or evil, called for instant communication. Let my delay stand excused; I had certain matters to be settled with myself that morning. My feet had to learn a new kind of movement, and my thoughts a new sequence; I was as a child learning to walk and think before I could take my place on equal terms with new companions. One incident of my walk struck me by way of humour and discovery. I had often strolled into bookshops toward evening, and had remarked upon the cold discourtesy with which my presence was regarded. Now I knew the reason; I had come at the clerk's hour, and the keen eyes of discriminating shopmen had recognised my low estate. I came now under altered auspices. To shop at three in the afternoon is to give proof of leisure; behold, in the eyes of obsequious shopmen I had at once become a wealthy dilettante, nurturing the growth of an expensive library, and the rarest books were laid before me with an ingratiating smile. Let the man who would understand how much the estimates men take of us are based on wealth, or supposed wealth, make the brief experiment of shopping at the rich man's hour, instead of at the poor man's; he will be surprised to note the difference of the social atmosphere. A man's clothes may be poor enough, and his appearance contemptible, but if he will shop at the hour when all the drudges are at work, no one will take him for a drudge. I will confess it gave me pleasure to note this change of estimate. I seemed to taste the first privilege of a freeman, when a pursy bookseller took from a glass case certain expensive books on Art, and drew my attention, with subtle deference to my judgment, to the merits of the pictures they contained. I may as well confess at once, that so intoxicated was I with the new respect that greeted me, that I even bought one of these volumes, which I did not need, and certainly could not afford. It was a weakness and a folly, no doubt; but how could I tell my obsequious friend that I paid my guinea not for anything he sold me, but as a sort of first footing on my entrance to the realm of freedom? I might have spent it much worse, for I bought my self-respect with it.

The sight of my doorstep brought me to my bearings, for a man's own doorstep is a rare corrective of disordered fancies. The fact I had to communicate was briefly this; That I had lost 250 pounds per annum, against which I had 50 pounds to show by way of compensation. Women, I have long noticed—or women of the best kind, I ought to add—have much more genius in finance than men. They have a much keener sense of the use of money; an excellent thing in women when it does not deteriorate into cheese-paring and sordid parsimony. They, being primitive and unsophisticated creatures, are unacquainted with the lax morals of the cheque-book; a pound is just twenty shillings to them, and each shilling is an entity, and each is spent with an indomitable aim to get the most out of it. How would my wife regard the definite disappearance of five thousand shillings? Not with levity, I knew; and I thought it best to say nothing of that guinea volume on the *Tombs of the Etruscans*. The *Tombs of the Etruscans* would have meant to her three pairs of boots; and I wished that I might conceal it in mine. A wise bishop once argued that marriage was ordained not for man's pleasure, but his discipline; I believe that he was not far wrong. It is no use disputing the fact that the married man is always in danger of the judgment; and it is only by some form of bribery that he can hope to escape being cast in damages. I resolved on bribery, and made my cheque the bribe. Here said I, was present wealth, let us be content. The plea was not received with instant favour, but it was not wholly ineffectual. By the time we sat down to supper that night we had all attained to cheerfulness. It was a meal of some tenuity, not calculated to lie heavy on the stomach; for, said Charlotte, 'If we have to begin high thinking and plain living, we can't begin too early.' The only load on my digestion that night was the *Tombs of the Etruscans*.

It says much for the steadfastness of our convictions, that in this new crisis of affairs the old resolution to seek a country life passed unquestioned. What to another had seemed calamity appeared to us opportunity. When the daily paper came next morning, it was not to the columns where commerce chronicles its wants that my eye turned, but to the much more engaging columns where lands and houses were advertised for sale. This part of the newspaper had long ago attracted me by its fine air of surreptitious romance. My mind had often been kept aglow for a whole day by some seductive advertisement of cottages 'situate amid pine-woods,' or farmhouses, all complete, even to the styes and kennels, which by all accounts were to be given away. One such advertisement I particularly remember for a kind of insane generosity which pervaded it. It described at length a farmhouse, 'stone-built and covered with ivy' (observe the very definite sense of the picturesque conveyed in this phrase), containing ten rooms, commanding pleasant views of a well-wooded country, together with a large orchard, and one hundred and fifty acres of freehold land, the whole of which might be purchased for 750 pounds; and, added the advertiser, 'the furniture at present in the house is included in the price.' I do not know where this terrestrial Paradise existed; I believe it was in Essex; but I often regretted that I made no effort to discover it.

However, the morning paper, if it contained no paragraph comparable with this in point of style and seduction, certainly did appear singularly rich in Paradises. Philanthropists, disguised as land-agents, contended eagerly with one another through many columns of advertisements, offering a reluctant world all the advantages of rural happiness on what appeared merely nominal terms. It appeared that they did not even want the money, which they mentioned only in a kind of gentlemanly whisper; pay them but 100 pounds in sound cash, and the rest might stand at mortgage upon easy terms for an indefinite period! One might have imagined that the whole of rural England was depopulated; that Eden itself had been cut up into building lots; that, in fact, the land-agent was subsidised by a paternal government to persuade the townsman to turn landed proprietor on terms which even the squatter in new lands would regard as generous.

The reality I soon found to be entirely different. The moment I set about the deliberate business of finding a cottage I made a series of surprising discoveries which I will now relate.

In the first place, I found that many of these much vaunted farmhouses were situated in districts utterly destitute of beauty, and even desolate. One specimen may stand for the whole. I omit the particulars of the advertisement, which was drawn up in the usual style; but I must say, in justice to its author, that when I interviewed him in his city office he did what he could to discourage too abundant hope. He did not go the length of admitting his description false, but he told me drily that 'I had better see the thing for myself.' An hour's journey found me on the Essex flats. There was a bright sky and a brisk wind, but nothing could disguise the featureless monotony of the far-stretched landscape. The train put me down at a roadside station where a dogcart waited my arrival. I drove through a small village of mean, red-brick houses, and soon found myself in the open country. My driver made but one remark during the four-mile journey.

'You be come to see Dawes' farm?' he said.

I admitted the fact.

'There's a-many has come,' he replied. 'You be the twenty-first I have drove. An' they all be uncommon glad to get away agen.'

'Why?' I asked.

'You'll soon find out.'

With that he lit his pipe and smoked stolidly. I was not long in comprehending the reason of his reticence. Dawes' farm may once have been a comfortable residence, but when I saw it it was a mildewed, rat-haunted ruin. It stood upon a piece of redeemed marsh-land, and the salt damp of the marsh had eaten into its very vitals. The wainscots were discoloured, the walls oozed, and part of the roof was broken. There had once been a garden; that, like the rest, was a ruin. The land was there no doubt, fifty acres said the advertisement, but it was treeless, bleak, flat, covered with coarse grass, and cut up by muddy watercourses. To have lived in the house at all it must have been rebuilt, and even then nothing could have made it a cheerful place of residence. There was no water-supply that I could discover, unless half a dozen butts that took the drippings of the roof represented it. The orchard had long ago gone back to barbarism. It appeared that the place had been deserted for half a dozen years. I did not wonder. The only wonder was that it had ever been inhabited.

'Ah,' repeated my driver, 'there's a-many as comes an' looks, an' they all be uncommon glad to get away agen.'

I subscribed to the common sentiment. Never did that infinite diapason which we call the roar of London sound so sweet, never did those long, lighted, busy streets seem so habitable, as on that night when I returned from my casual inspection of Dawes' farm.

The memory of Dawes' farm taught me that if I was to live in the country some charm of outlook was indispensable to my content. Mountains, a lake, a wood, a running river—some delicate effect of scenery, some concourse of elements, either in themselves or in their combination beautiful—these I must have if I would be happy. They were as necessary to me as my daily bread. But here I made a second disquieting discovery; there was not a part of England which could be justly described as beautiful that was not already occupied in the degree of its accessibility. I thought of Surrey; I visited it and found myself in a superior Cockney Paradise. Half a dozen men of genius had in an inadvertent moment advertised the pure air of the Surrey highlands, and by the time I came upon the scene trim villas had sprung up by hundreds, and wealth was already in possession. The merest cottage in this favoured district provoked keen contest in the auction-room. Indeed, in the true sense, there were no cottages; they had been transformed, added to, rebuilt, till only a remnant of their primitive rusticity remained. It was the same everywhere. I was too late by twenty years in this kind of quest.

I had been led to believe by various social writers that the villages of England were depopulated. According to these fallacious chroniclers the country abounded in cottages and even small manor-houses from which the inhabitants had fled. I can only say I never found it so. A deserted roadside cottage I often found, but there were obvious reasons for its desolation. Sometimes it was so far from other houses, or any centre of congregated life, that it must have been difficult, and almost impossible, for any one residing in it to obtain the common necessaries of life. More commonly it was deserted because it was falling into ruin. But no sooner did I reach a real village than I found every house in occupation. The usual complaint was lack of accommodation. Hence rents were by no means low, and the contest for houses was vehement. If the village had real beauties of its own—a cluster of thatched and dormer-windowed cottages, properties valuable to the artist—one was sure to come upon immediate evidence of the cockney invasion. What I thought a barn would as like as not prove a studio, and it was no farmer who lived at the pleasant, yellow-washed farmhouse amid the rose-garden, but 'a gentleman from London.' And we had but to go a little way down some shady lane to find a glaring board announcing building land for lease, and from some local agent one obtained particulars of the exact kind of house which the investor would be permitted to build upon the site.

It will be said that this was not the country proper, nor was it, for London has annexed every place within fifty miles of Charing Cross. But in the country proper a new difficulty met me: not only were there no empty cottages, but landowners stuck to their acres with such jealous obstinacy that they refused to sell a rood of land for a cottage on any terms whatever. I will give one example, which may be taken as typical. There was a Welsh valley where I had once spent a summer holiday, exquisitely retired and beautiful—a dozen miles from the nearest railway. Beyond the green strath, with its few white cottages and farms, rose on every side the wide hills, with Snowdon towering over all like a dome. The hillside land had but a prairie value. It had never been cultivated. A few sheep strayed over it; but for months together no human foot trod its heather, or wandered by its vociferous cascades. One would have supposed that had any one offered to build a house on these solitary hillsides, the owner of the land would have been only too glad to have fostered a folly that would have proved remunerative to himself. On the contrary, the two great landowners of the district stuck to every inch of soil as if it had been sown with gold. The land was quite useless, as I have said. It might have been worth three pounds an acre—yet they refused fifty. They would not even let on lease. Nor could it be pretended that the scenery would have lost any element of its charm by a cottage that would have been scarcely observed on those vast slopes of Snowdon. Jealous obstinacy, the desire to keep intact their own, the desire to keep out all intruders—this was the temper of the landowners. They did all they could to harass their existing tenants. A tenant whose family had increased so that his cottage was as overcrowded as a tenement in Spitalfields, had to plead long before he was allowed to add a couple of rooms to his cottage, even when he did so at his own expense. Often enough he was refused so harshly, that he was constrained to seek a house in some other district. Yet, in all that valley, which was five miles long by two in breadth, there were not two hundred houses; and there rose around them the unpopulated hillside, where a host of people might have lived in health, and where, indeed, men had once lived, as was witnessed by the roofless gables which here and there rose among the heather.

It seems to me that in this state of things there is a monstrous injustice. There is no law to compel these gentlemen to sell land, and there is no public sentiment that can affect them. They are the complete despots of the countryside. If a man does not like their domination, he leaves the district; he knows that it is vain to resist it. In this way many rural districts are depopulated, or kept under-populated, simply to gratify the selfish temper of a great proprietor. It is not as though he lived in the district, and wished to keep its beauties secret to himself; often enough he visits it so rarely that his face is not known among his tenants. No; but he must have everything to himself; he must round off his estate; he must look from his park on nothing which is not his; for your rural Ahab could not sleep with a Naboth's little vineyard even a mile away. It is useless to tell him that the land you want is waste natural land, on which you propose to confer value; he prefers that it shall be valueless, rather than that it shall be yours. Before population can be re-distributed to the advantage of town and country alike, this difficulty must be overcome. It can only be overcome by drastic legislation. Compulsory purchase, regulated by an equitable land court, is the only remedy; and it is hard that Irishmen should have, and grumble over, privileges which their English brethren would receive with open arms.

Such were some of the discoveries which I made when I came to the real business of finding a humble country residence. In my ignorance and inexperience it had seemed the easiest thing in the world. After a fortnight of experiment I began to think it was the hardest.

CHAPTER VII

I FIND MY COTTAGE

In the meantime a circumstance had occurred which was of great importance to me. Some enterprising spirits had started a new weekly local paper, and—*mirabile dictu*—they actually contemplated a literary page! With a faith in suburban culture, so unprecedented as to be almost sublime, these daring adventurers proposed giving their readers reviews of books, literary gossip, and general information about the doings of eminent writers. They offered the work to me at the modest honorarium of two pounds a week, and were willing to give me a three years' agreement. They were frank enough to acknowledge that their journal was likely to die of 'superiority to its public,' long before the three years were over; but, barring this disaster, they gave me assurance of regular employment. This was the very thing for me. One could write about books anywhere. I thankfully closed with the offer and began to study the ha'-penny evening papers with assiduity, in order to learn the craft of manufacturing biographies of living authors.

The greatest of all questions was thus settled: I should not starve. But the question of a local habitation remained as difficult as ever. I went upon wild-goose chases innumerable; was the victim of every kind of chance hint; gathered fallacious information from garrulous third-class passengers on many railways; confided my case to carters and rural postmen, who played upon my innocence with genial malice; stayed so long at village public-houses without visible motive that I incurred the suspicion of the local constabulary, and on one memorable occasion found myself identified with a long watched-for robber of local hen-roosts. When I dropped upon some quaint village that, from a pictorial point of view, seemed to offer all that I desired, I found my tale, that I wished to settle in it, universally derided. No one could conceive any sane person as being desirous of living in a village; the design seemed wholly unaccountable to people who themselves would have been only too glad to live in towns.

That I came from London was against me, It seemed to these village Daniels barely possible that I was honest, and quite certain that I cloaked some base designs under an innocent inquiry for empty cottages. The little black bag in which I carried my lunch on these excursions was the object of extraordinary hypotheses. At one time I was believed to be selling tracts, at another time, tea; once I was suspected of being an itinerant anarchist, doing a brisk business in infernal machines. Landladies, who had lavished smiles upon me when they supposed me an ordinary pedestrian in search of the picturesque, gave me the cold shoulder when I began to explain my genuine intentions. They sometimes treated me with such a mixture of aversion and alarm that it was plain they doubted not only my sincerity but my sanity. The travelling artist they knew, the pedlar, the insurance agent, and the cockney beanfeaster; but the stranger who desired permanent neighbourship with them they knew not; him they treated as a lunatic at large. If the papers had chanced to be full at this time of the doings of some flagrant murderer flying from justice, which fortunately for me they were not, I have little doubt that these amiable villagers would have delivered me up to the police without scruple, and have chuckled over their sagacity.

The thing was amusing enough, and yet it had a certain serious significance. It was a striking illustration of the way in which the growth of cities had perverted even the rural mind. I had thoughts of writing an article on *The Reluctant Villagers,* and a very good article I could have made of it; for I found hardly any one who was a villager by choice. A village might appear fair as Paradise to the casual eye; but closer inspection always revealed the serpent of discontent among the flowers. Where every outward object breathed of rest, there was universal restlessness among the people. The common ambition of all the younger generation was to get to London by almost any means, and in almost any capacity. There was not a household that had not children or relatives in London. The young ploughman went to London as a carter or ostler; the milkmaid as a servant. The village carpenter was invariably a middle-aged or an old man, secretly despised by his apprentice, if he had one, for his contentment with his lot. One saw very few young people in the village street, except mere children. The universal complaint was that life was dull. There were no libraries or reading-rooms; no concerts or entertainments; even the innocuous penny-reading had died out. Nor were there cricket clubs, or any organised system of sport, except in isolated cases. Here and there a modern-minded clergyman had recognised the need of recreation in his parishioners, and had done something to provide for it; but he was an exception. Hence it happened that the public-house was the common centre of the village life: it was the poor man's club, and it was used less for purposes of social intercourse than for the discussing of racing odds.

Artists have often painted village politicians in earnest confabulation in an oak-pannelled inn-parlour. I can only say that, so far as my experience went, I found the village politician quite extinct. The sort of talk I heard in village bar-rooms was inane and contemptible to the last degree, and it never once touched on politics. Nor, as a rule, was there any trace of that leaven of superior intelligence which comes from a fusion of the classes. All the landlords were practically non-resident. They knew nothing of their tenants; and that pleasant intercourse between hall and cottage which poets and novelists depict, rarely happened. Once a year, perhaps, and for a few weeks only, the blinds of the Hall windows were drawn up; carriages rolled through the park gates; young ladies, bright in Bond Street toilets, flashed like deities upon the village street; my Lady Bountiful left a quarter of a pound of tea at half a dozen cottages; and then the whole vision faded like an unsubstantial pageant. The blinds were drawn down again, the lodge-keeper went to sleep, and the monotonies of life submerged everything like a wave. The clergyman alone remained as the symbol of a fuller life, sometimes doing his duty with intelligence, sometimes not; but the case was rare where any definite attempt was made to uplift the village community by the infusion of any intellectual interest, any sense of Art, or any care for honest sport. And here lies the whole secret of the discontent of villages; their inhabitants are conscious of unjust deprivations in their lot; and if they remain villagers, it is rather from lethargy than love.

Were I to describe all the places I visited in search of a habitation, my list would be interminable. I have given one example in Dawes' Farm; let me give one other, as illustrating another kind of difficulty in my quest.

On an exquisite morning in June I found myself climbing the long chalk hills that lie northward of the Thames valley. At every step the air became more pure and sparkling; and while in the hazy lowlands not a leaf stirred, here a brisk and gusty breeze was blowing. The road ran through high chalk banks, like a railway cutting, and I have since found that Roman soldiers used it in the days of Caesar. At the height of three hundred feet authentic forest scenery began. Here the elms ceased, and enormous woods of beech took their place. The turf was of the greenest, the solitude intense, the air exhilarating; and never had I so admired the lace-like delicacy of foliage which distinguishes the beech, for never had I seen it in such mass or such perfection. The house I sought stood at fully eight hundred feet above sea-level, on a carpet of soft turf, round which the forest rose like a wall. Never did place look so sweetly habitable; it was a kind of green hermitage in the woods, inimitably quiet, warmed by clearest sunlight, cooled by freshest winds. Here, said I, at last is my much sought El Dorado; nor did the cottage, when I came to it, belie my hopes. It was a true woodland cottage, an intimate part and parcel of the scenery. It had been recently inhabited by a man of letters, a poet and a dreamer; and a fitter spot to dream in eye never rested on.

My enthusiasm rose as I drew nearer to it, There was a warm, homely compactness about it, as of a nest among the trees. The forest turf came to the very gate; a young orchard of five hundred trees lay to the southward of the house, a green paddock to the northward; and, as my advertisement informed me, the entire price of this eligible freehold property was five hundred pounds! Why, then, was its possessor so eager to be quit of it? I walked round the house, went through its rooms, took the view from various windows, already treating it as mine, and it was long before I came upon the cause. That cause was not its remoteness or its solitude; it was lack of water. There was no well, and to have sunk a well would have been costly. The only water-supply was the rain-water from the roofs. Men can laugh at a good many deprivations, but deprivation of water is a serious business. I found upon inquiry that the nearest spring was two miles away. In time of drought—and in this high district summer drought was normal—it was this or nothing. Water was then sold by the bucket, nor was it easy to find any one to fetch and carry for you. I had no mind to condemn myself to drink the droppings of a roof for life, nor to perform my ablutions by the aid of a teacup and a saucer. The place, for all its beauty, was plainly uninhabitable as the Sahara. A camel might have lived there with content; it was no place for a family used to the delights of tubbing. I had remarked in the owner of the house a certain elementary lack of linen; the cause was now explained. I think his only method of attaining cleanliness must have been by what is called 'the dry air process.'

This adventure lives in my memory, not only because it had delightful elements, but because it was the last of a long series, which might have been called more truthfully misadventures. For an exhilarating month I scoured the neighbourhood of London, living in a happy fever of enterprise and hope, but without result. July came, and my problem was still unsolved. I had already given notice to terminate the tenancy of my house in London, and there seemed a fair prospect that September would find me homeless. At my present height of good spirits I cannot say that even this prospect dismayed me. If the worst came to the worst I meant to take to the road in one of those convenient vans much used by travelling hawkers. I had long envied the extraordinary snugness of those itinerant habitations; to be a Dr. Marigold seemed the happiest of fates; rent free, and finally delivered from tax-collectors and their tribe, I might yet roam the world as a superior kind of vagrant. I knew indeed a young friend of mine who had adopted this very life. He sold tracts and Bibles upon village greens, and I promise you no mansion had a warmer glow of comfort than the interior of his yellow van when the lamp was lit at night for supper. He has since found his way to a lonely missionary station in Peru; but he has often told me that he was never happier than when he played the part of pious gipsy on the village greens of England. At a pinch I thought that I could do what he had done; it was a romantic trade, and a new *Lavengro* might be written on it.

But whatever dreams of permanent and dedicated vagrancy I might entertain, manifestly my first duty was to find a cottage if I could. At last, and almost by accident, I came on what I wanted. I had gone to the Lake District in the month of August, and one day I struck into a lonely road to the north-west of Buttermere. Half an hour's walk brought me to a tiny hamlet beside a rushing stream, and here, for the first time in all my wanderings, I found a genuine deserted cottage. To speak by the book there were two cottages exactly similar, covered by a single roof. They stood upon a gentle slope; a group of pines formed a shelter from the north, the moorland rose behind them, and the river sang through a contiguous glen. My first glance told me that they had not long been out of occupation. They showed no marks of dilapidation, and the little gardens, though weed-grown, gave signs of recent care. A woman whom I met told me their history. They had long been inhabited by two families, father and son. A few months previously these families had sailed for Canada. No one had applied for the cottages, for in that part work was scarce, and the foundries and shipyards on the coast drew away the younger population. The rent—it seemed incredible—was two shillings a week. The woman yielded to what she thought my idle curiosity, and brought me the keys. Each cottage contained four rooms, and the two could easily be thrown into one. They were dry and water-tight, the walls whitewashed and clean, the woodwork sound and well cared for. I sat down upon the sun-warmed bank beside the gate and thought. Here was solitude indeed; a dozen neighbours in all, simple labouring folk:

> The silence that is in the starry sky,
> The sleep that is among the lonely hills.

Here, too, was beauty in excess; a glen untrodden by the feet of tourists, moorland and pine-wood, a stream that lifted up a cheerful voice, hills and mountains of delightful form and colour, and not far away the silver gleam of lakes. In all external features it was my dream come true, and the deep-bosomed woman at my side, with her face of rosy, placid health, was herself the proof of how lightly the wings of time passed over this haunt of ancient peace.

I suppose that no one ever approaches the realisation of his hopes without a kind of fear. In those imaginary dramas which we invent and rehearse perpetually in the silent theatre of our own minds, we always take care that we get the best of the situation and the dialogue. The dramas of real life are apt to end differently. The coveted occasion finds us incapable; a baffling scepticism of our own powers leaves us impotent; the part that ran so easily, with such unanimous applause, when we were both the dramatist and the actor, suddenly bristles with a hundred unsuspected difficulties. For the first time, as I sat on that sunny bank, I began to ask myself whether I could really play the part I had so long desired to play. Could I reconcile myself to seclusion so entire? Would not this weight of utter silence grow heavier than I could bear? It was not always June, I told myself, and there were days of lashing rain, grey skies, and 'death-dumb autumn dripping' fog to think of. The vision of lighted streets and bustling crowds, the warm contiguity of numbers, the long lines of windows all aglow at evening, the genial stir and tumult of congregated life, took masterful possession of my mind. Could I bear to relinquish the familiar scene? A thousand threads of use and habit bound me to it, each in itself as light as gossamer, but the whole tough as cords of steel. I foresaw that I had underestimated the ease of my deliverance. It would require a strength of consistent resolution of which perhaps I was not capable. It was but too likely that I should be one of those who put their hand to the plough and look back, a reluctant recruit of a cause that won my faith, but could not win my will. This would be not only fatal to my peace, it would make me despicable in my own eyes, which is the worst of all calamities that man can suffer.

Such a distress of mind was natural; yet I think that behind it all my thought was firm and clear. What I had proposed to do for twenty years I must do, or attempt to do, if I would retain my self-respect. I might become despicable to myself by failure in my task, but I should be much more despicable by never trying to accomplish it. In that half-hour of meditation the die was cast. I had come to my predestined battlefield. I must here be triumphant or defeated; in any case I must attempt the conflict.

The decision restored, as by a stroke of magic, all my good spirits. I examined my two cottages again with an eye less critical, more kindly, more urbane. I saw with how few touches they could be transformed into a habitation suited to my needs. With the two main rooms thrown into one I should have a spacious living-room; the two gardens would compose an admirable lawn; roses should grow against the walls, warm-hued creepers frame the upper windows; it should become a lodge in Eden. Then there was the air, the view, the company of the silent mountains and the singing stream. Here was my theatre, my orchestra, my concert-room. The woman who was my guide took me into her own cottage for a cup of tea, and I was struck with its homely air of comfort. An oak dresser, covered with blue ware such as is common in these parts, filled one wall; an oak chest of drawers another; there was a broad-seated oak settle by the fire; all solid, of a good design, and polished to a deep brown by use and industry. The floor was red brick; flowers lined the windows; and everything was clean as hands could make it. I saw my house furnished on the same plan, and it pleased me. A recollection crossed my mind, curious and most fantastic at such a time, of a certain room in one of the show-houses in London, furnished entirely in the French style. I recalled the console tables of old gilt, the brocaded couch, and the gilded chairs which no one dared to sit upon; and I confess that I preferred this habitable cottage-room. There was something satisfying in its plainness; a sense of something honest and intimately right; a suggestion of solid worth and homely ease. My spirits had already been restored by my decision; they were now invigorated to the point of joy, for I saw the concrete emblems, as it were, of the beauty which is found in true simplicity.

The next day I returned to the spot accompanied by my wife and my two boys. We made a new and elaborate inspection of the two cottages. In the afternoon the landlord, a neighbouring farmer, met us. He was a dales-man born and bred, shrewd, much given to silence, but with a plenitude of genial good sense. He began by being somewhat suspicious of us after the usual country fashion. When he at last understood the sincerity and novelty of our intentions, he treated us with a kind of fatherly derision, which had no hint of impoliteness or impertinence in it. 'It will na do, I'm thinking,' he said, several times. When he saw us persistent, and that our persistence grew in the ratio of his dissuasion, he said, just as though he were talking to wayward children, 'Well, a wilful man maun have his way. As for my bit of cottages, ye're welcome to them, an' I'll ask no rent till ye've been in them long enough to know your own minds better. They're of no worth to me, an' I'll be your debtor for living in them. If ye want to pull them aboot, ye'll do it at your own expense, I'm willing. Later on, if ye care to stay, you and me'll fix a rent, an' I gie ye ma word it shall na be more than ten pund a year. I'll help ye too if ye'll let me. I can find ye a man as 'll do all the little jobs you want done, an' glad to do it. As for fishing, the stream's yours, an' I would na say but what ye might get some shooting too. But ye'll tire of it, ye'll tire of it,' he concluded, with a grave smile.

With that he handed us the keys. He then shook our hands with the melancholy air of a man who says farewell to friends embarked upon a perilous adventure, and strode away across the heather, stopping once to wave his hand to us as if in wise dissuasion.

So Mahomet might have stood above Damascus when he said, 'My Paradise is not there,' and yet Damascus was a Paradise all the same.

CHAPTER VIII

BUYING HAPPINESS

We are all children, and in nothing so much perhaps as in the kind of delight we take in any form of building. The architectural efforts of a child with a box of bricks or a heap of sand explain the Tower of Babel, the Pyramids, and the Golden House of Nero. House-building unites the ideal with the real more thoroughly than any other human employment. What can there be more delightful than to see that which you have dreamed grow into tangible and enduring form? No wonder the rich man builds himself 'a lordly pleasure-house'; it is a kind of practical poetry which he can understand. Were there only millionaires enough to go round all architects would be wealthy, for building is a kind of material art admirably suited to men of material intelligence.

The weeks which followed the acquisition of my two deserted cottages were the most delightful I have ever spent. First of all, there was the question of structural alterations to be considered. In my opinion the living-room of the house is the chief consideration. It should be a *room to live in*, the focus of the whole life of the household. For this reason it should be large and airy, covering the whole site of the house as nearly as possible. One large room is infinitely to be preferred to two or three small rooms; it is healthier, and much more cheerful. Space and air are most needed in the room which is most in use. It is of no consequence that the bedrooms should be small; one's active hours are not spent in them, and a window left wide open summer and winter will provide an ample supply of oxygen in the smallest chamber. What can be more absurd than the arrangement of a modern London villa? It is usually cut up by partition walls into a number of small rooms, not more than one of which is in constant use. Pretension takes the place of comfort. Mrs. Grundy must have a 'drawing-room' or die! It is a kind of holiest of holies, too beautiful for normal occupation, full of gimcrack chairs that cannot be sat upon, and decorative futilities which give it the aspect of a miscellaneous stall at a 'rummage sale.' Such a room is very well as a _with_drawing-room, its proper use; but as a room into which no one withdraws it is absurd. As I expected to keep no company, and needed no room into which to withdraw, I was able to get rid of this apartment. Moreover, in a very small house, common sense demanded that every room should be really and thoroughly used.

Fortunately the fireplaces of my two cottages were against the outer or gable ends, and not against the partition wall, as is commonly the case. I had only to remove this partition wall, supporting the ceiling by a strong beam, and I had a room about twenty-four long by fifteen in breadth. At the back of this room were two small kitchens, only one of which was needed. By widening the doorway leading to one of them to double its breadth, I gained another room about ten feet square. This made my library, by which I mean not a room in which I ever sat, but a room entirely devoted to the housing of my books. I had the walls entirely lined with books, making and staining the bookshelves with my own hands. Across the widened doorway from which the door had been removed hung a warm curtain, so that it was to all intents and purposes a part of my living-room. I took infinite and almost childish delight in the arrangement of this living-room. I had brought not a single article of domestic furniture with me from London. Such furniture as I had—chairs, tables, couch, sideboard, and so forth—would have looked out of place in the country, and moreover it was better economy to sell them. I sold them very well in a London auction-room, getting almost as much as they cost me. With the money thus received in my pocket I went to a neighbouring market town where there happened to be a shop that dealt in old furniture. For less than ten pounds I bought an excellent oaken gate-table, half a dozen serviceable oak chairs, a couple of fine carved chests, and a corner cupboard. My oak dresser and settle, each good specimens of serviceable cottage furniture, cost me thirty-seven shillings at a country auction. I found that even at these modest prices I had paid too much. Oaken furniture was common in these parts, and had little value. When a church was restored, or an old house re-constructed, large quantities of old oak were literally thrown away. Thus, at a merely nominal expense I acquired enough carved oak to fit together into a handsome fireplace, and later on the pews of a church came in for oak panelling.

Let me now picture my living-room as it was about four months after I took possession. It was entirely oak panelled to a height of nine feet, above which about a foot of white-washed wall showed, forming a plain frieze. The fireplace at one end of the room was built in with carved oak; what had been the corresponding fireplace at the other end of the room was turned into a cupboard, with plain oak doors. The room had three old-fashioned leaded windows opening outward. Two were original, one had been added—the centre window taking the place of the gap left by the destroyed partition wall. My oak chests, dresser and cupboard, constituted the furniture of the room. The library, curtained off with a plain curtain of crimson plush, adjoined; the kitchen door opened at the east corner of the room. The windows faced due south. The room therefore was always sunny. The floor-boards were stained, and covered by two or three cheap rugs. Flowers were at the windows, a vase of flowers always on the table. The fireplace was open, for I had removed the ugly modern grate, substituting for it a low hearth of red brick with iron dogs, on which wood could be burned. This room, with the adjoining library, was the great feature of my little house.

The other rooms in the house required no alteration; fresh whitewash and wall-papers soon transformed them; and although they were small, they were not devoid of charm. When my scheme of adaptation was complete I found myself possessed of a house containing one beautiful living-room, a small library, a kitchen, and four good bedrooms. My bill for labour, including the mason's work in the removal of the partition wall, the building of a new window, and the laying of a fresh hearth; the carpenter's work in fitting my oak, and various minor repairs, amounted in all to about twelve pounds. The cost of my furniture, including the oak panelling in the living-room, and all that was needed for the bedrooms, was about fifty pounds, against which I had to set thirty-eight pounds, received from the sale of my superfluous effects in London. If I added to these sums the general expenses of removal, the carriage and cartage of my goods, and so forth, which I reckoned at ten pounds, I found that the cost of my exodus and new tenancy had been as follows:—

       L. s. d.
By expenses of removal 10 0 0
By alterations and labour 12 0 0
By cost of furniture for living-room
 and four bedrooms 50 0 0
       ―――――
      L72 0 0
Against which, by sale of goods in
 London 38 0 0

It was in the end of August when I took my house; by the beginning of December I had completed my work upon it. The gardens in front of the house had been levelled, and covered with the finest mountain turf. The walls had been colour-washed a warm yellow, and all the window-frames painted white. For three months every hour had been busy, and not the least blessing of my toil was that it had brought me a degree of physical vigour such as I had never yet enjoyed. How different were my sensations when I woke in the morning now from those which I had known in London! In London the hour of rising had invariably found me languid and reluctant. I woke with the sense of a load upon me, and I dreaded the long grey day. I see now that these sensations were not so much mental as physical. I had not mental buoyancy simply because I was deficient in physical vitality. But at Thornthwaite I woke eager for the day. The first sounds that greeted me through the open window were the songs of the birds, the sea-like diapason of the wind in the elm-trees on the lawn, and the animating song of the river in the glen. The weather during the whole of that autumn was extraordinarily fine. After a week of equinoctial storm in the end of September, the weather settled into exquisite repose. Day succeeded day, calm, bright, sunny. It was as warm as August, but with all the tonic freshness of autumn. November, usually a month of misery in London, was here delightful. The year died slowly, amid the pomp of crimson leaves and bronzed bracken. For the first time I understood that it is bliss to be alive. Like the child whom Wordsworth celebrates, I felt my life in every limb. There was no goading of dull powers to unwelcome tasks; energy ran free, like the mountain-stream at my door, and the zest of life was strong in me.

I never came downstairs into my living-room without a sense of new delight. How beautiful, how sweetly habitable it looked in the morning sunshine! Any one living in a city, who immediately on rising enters the room which he has used overnight, has noticed the peculiar staleness of the atmosphere. It is not exactly a noxious atmosphere; there is no palpable unpleasant odour in it, but it is used up, it is stale. He will also notice the dust which rests on everything. In a city the daily grinding of millions of wheels over thousands of miles of roads fills the air with an acrid, almost impalpable powder, which finds its way even through closed windows and settles upon everything. In my London house I could not take up a book without soiled fingers. Even books which were protected by glass doors, and papers shut up in drawers, did not escape this filthy powder, composed of the fine-ground dust and excrement of the London streets. If I wiped a picture with a white silk handkerchief, a black stain showed itself upon the handkerchief, and this in spite of the most careful efforts to keep the house clean. I suppose Londoners get used to dirt, as eels are said to get used to skinning. They spend their time in washing their hands, but with the most transient gain of cleanliness. No one knows how filthy London is till he begins to notice how much longer window-curtains, household draperies, and personal linen keep clean in the country. I should not like to be called an old maid, but I confess to an old-maidish care for cleanliness. Untidiness in books or papers would not distress me, but dirt is a real distress; and if it be old-maidish to fight a continual battle with dirt, to scour and polish and dust, content with nothing less than immaculate purities of polished surface, then I suppose I am an old maid, and I count it to myself for righteousness.

Amid the many miseries of cities, this no doubt is but a minor misery, but the relief which I experienced in deliverance from it was disproportionately great. The purity and freshness of the atmosphere, the corresponding cleanliness of all I touched in the house, were delightful to me, and added to my self-respect. The clean, aromatic air passed like a ceaseless lustration through every room of the house. The very bed-linen, bleached in the open air, had acquired the fragrance of mountain thyme and lavender. I did not need to climb the hill to find the pine-woods; they grew round the very table where I ate. Four walls and a roof gave me shelter, yet I lived in the open air all the time.

Then there was also the silence, at first so strange as to be almost oppressive, but later on sweeter than music. It was at early morning and nightfall that this silence was most intense. On a still night one could almost hear the earth move, and fancy that the stars diffused a gentle crackling noise as of rushing flame. The fall of an acorn in a pine wood startled the ear like an explosion. The river also was discerned as having a definite rhythm of its own. It ran up and down a perpetual scale, like a bird singing. What had seemed a heavy confused sound of falling water resolved itself into regular harmonies, which could have been written down in musical notation. At times there was also in the air the sense of breathing. On a dark night, standing at my door, I had the sense of a great heart that beat in the obscurity, of a bosom that rose and fell, of a pulse as regular as a clock. I think that the ear must have recovered a fine sensitiveness, normal to it under normal conditions, but lost or dulled amid the deafening roar of towns. It is scarcely an exaggeration when poets speak of hearing the grass grow; we could hear it, no doubt, if the ear were not stunned by more violent sounds.

It is probable that mere increase of vitality in itself is sufficient to account for this new delicacy of the physical senses. The senses adapt themselves to their environment. An example of this is found in the absence of what is called long sight among city children. Having no extensive horizon constantly before the eye, the power of discerning distant objects gradually decays. On the contrary a child brought up upon the African veldt, where he is daily confronted with almost infinite distances, acquires what seems to be an almost preternatural sharpness of vision. It is the same with hearing. The savage can distinguish sounds which are entirely inaudible to the civilised man. The footfall of his enemy, the beat of a horse's hoofs, the movement of a lion in the jungle, are heard at what appear impossible distances. I do not seek to offer any absolute explanation of these phenomena as regards myself, but I state the fact that in returning to a natural life I found a remarkable quickening of my physical senses. As my eye became accustomed to the wide moorland prospects I found myself increasingly able to discriminate distant objects. Flowers that had seemed to me to smell pretty much alike, now had distinct fragrances. I knew when I woke in the morning from which direction the wind came, by its odour; the wind from the moorland brought the scent of heather and wild thyme, the wind from the glen the scent of water.

It was the same with sound. Properly speaking there is no such thing as silence in Nature. The silence, or what seems silence, is divisible into a multitude of minute sounds. Everything in Nature is toiling and straining at its task, the sap in the tree, the rock balanced on its bed of clay, the grass-blade pushing and urging its way toward the sun. And as there is no real silence, so there is no real solitude in a world where every atom is vigorously at work. Wordsworth's conception of Nature as a Presence becomes at once intelligible when we live close to the heart of Nature. Had Wordsworth lived in towns his poetry could never have been written, nor can its central conception of Nature as a Presence be understood by the townsman. I had often enough read the wonderful lines—

> And I have felt
> A presence that disturbs me with the joy
> Of elevated thoughts: a sense sublime
> Of something far more deeply interfused,
> Whose dwelling is the light of setting suns,
> And the round ocean, and the living air,
> And the blue sky, and in the mind of man

A motion and a spirit, that impels
All thinking things, all objects of all thought,
And rolls through all things.

But I never really understood them till I lived among scenes similar to those in which they were composed. And the organ by which they were interpreted was not the mind so much as the senses, quickened and invigorated by solitude. I presented a more sensitive surface to Nature, and the instant result was the perception of Nature as of something alive. In the silence of the night, as I stood at my door, I felt the palpitation of a real life around me; the sense, as I have said, of a breathing movement, of pulsation, of a beating heart, and then I knew that Wordsworth wrote with strict scientific accuracy, and not with vague mysticism as is commonly supposed, when he described Nature as a living Presence.

The sum of these sensations was for me a state of physical beatitude. I was often reminded of the grim confession of the poor wastrel, who, when asked where he lived, replied, 'I don't live, I linger.' I had never really lived; I had lingered. I had trodden the path of the days and years with reluctant feet. Now every daybreak was a new occasion of joy to me. I was rejuvenated not only in mind, but in the very core and marrow of my body. I had put myself in right relation to Nature; I had established contact, as electricians would say; and as a consequence all the electric current of Nature flowed through me, vitalising and quickening me in every nerve. Men who live in cities are but half alive. They mistake infinite contortion for life. Life consists in the efficient activity of every part of us, each part equally efficient, and moving in a perfect rhythm. For the first time, since I had been conscious of myself, I realised this entire efficiency.

Many times I had coveted what is called 'rude health,' but I had been led to believe that rude health implies lack of sensitiveness. I now found the reverse to be the case. Perfect health and perfect sensitiveness are the same thing. I felt, enjoyed, and received sensations more acutely simply because my health was perfect. It may be said that the sensations afforded by such a life as mine were not upon a grand scale. They were not to be compared with the acute and poignant sensations afforded—perhaps I should say inflicted—by a city. I can only say they were enough for me. All pleasures are relative, and the simplest pleasure is capable of affording as great delight as the rarest. The sight of a flower can produce as keen a pleasure as a Coronation pageant, and the song of a bird may become to the sensitive ear as fine a music as a sonata by Beethoven. May I not also say that the simplest pleasures are the most enduring, the commonest delights are the most invigorating, the form of happiness which is the most easily available is the best? The further we stray from Nature the harder are we to please, and he knows the truest pleasure who can find it in the simplest forms.

CHAPTER IX

HOW WE LIVED

The most common objection to country life is what is called its dulness. When I used to suggest to my town acquaintances the advantages of a holiday in purely rustic scenes, I was always met by the remark: 'Oh, there would be nothing to do there!' No doubt if a holiday is devoted to lounging, it is much more difficult to lounge at a solitary farm than at some crowded seaside resort. But my holidays in the country had never been of this description. I am constitutionally unfitted for a lounger. I like to have my days planned out, and to live them fully. A country holiday for me had always meant incessant occupation of one kind or another, fishing, climbing, boating, long cycling excursions, and an industrious endeavour to explore all scenes of interest within a reasonable compass. Now that I had come to live in the country, I felt more than ever the need of incessant occupation, for I fully realised that the worst enemy of human happiness is ennui.

During the first three months, while I was busy in getting settled, there was no danger of ennui. I was constantly interested, and I was constantly at work. I learned how to do carpentering and joiner's jobs with a fair proficiency; I dug nearly an acre of land at the back of my house with my own spade; made paths, and planted fruit trees; all the turf for my lawn I laid myself, with a few hours' assistance from a farm-hand; and there was no night when I did not go to bed with aching muscles and often with bruised hands. If my bill for labour was absurdly moderate, it was partly because I did so much myself.

For instance, I employed no one to hang papers or to whitewash ceilings or paint woodwork. With the willing help of my wife and my boys this was done with complete satisfaction. One result of these labours was the pride and love for our little homestead which they created. In modern civilised life we get too many things done for us, and this is not merely an economical but an ethical mistake. It is difficult to feel any real pride in a home which is the creation of other people. In a true state of civilisation no man will pay another to do what he can do himself. Not only does he preserve his independence by such a rule, but he creates a hundred new objects of interest for himself. The paper which I had hung with my own labour gave me a pleasure which a much finer paper hung by paid labour could not have given me. The lawn which I had laid with my own hands seemed more intimately mine than if I had paid some one else to make it. The more I reflect upon the matter the more am I convinced that one of the great curses of civilisation is the division of labour which makes us dependent upon other people to a degree which destroys individual efficiency. Thrown back upon himself as a dweller in a wilderness, any man of ordinary capacity soon develops efficiency for kinds of work which he would never have attempted in a city, simply because a city tempts him at every point to delegate his own proper toil to others. I can conceive of few things that would do more to create a genuine pride of home than to insist that no man should possess a house except by building it for himself, after the old primitive principle of the earliest social communities. To build thus is to mix sentiment with the mortar, and the house thus created is a place to which affections and memories cling; whereas the mere tenancy of a cube of rotten bricks, thrown together by the jerry-builder—of which we know no more than the amount of rent which is charged for it—is incapable of nourishing any sentiment, and is, in any case, not a home but a lodging.

This idea is no doubt chimerical; for in a vast city, where the great object is to escape starvation, no one has time to interest himself deeply in the kind of house he occupies, and still less has he the opportunity to build a house which is the expression of his own taste and labour. But in the country the idea is not only practicable, it is urgent. Independence is made necessary because there are fewer people on whom we can become dependent. I soon found that if I wanted potatoes and cabbages, I must grow them; if a pipe burst there was no plumber to mend it, I must mend it myself; and so through a long range of occupations, with which I had had no previous acquaintance. The immortal Captain Davis, of the *Sea Ranger*, remarks to the incompetent landsman Herrick, whom he has engaged as first mate on the *Farralone*, 'There ain't nothing *to* sailoring when you come to look it in the face,' and I am inclined to think that the observation is true of other things besides navigation. There is nothing in ordinary gardening, carpentering, or work about a house that any intelligent man cannot learn in a month by giving his mind to it. Intelligence, industry, and a deft hand will take any man of capacity through any of the ordinary employments of life with moderate credit, or at least without disgrace. When once the right handling of tools is learned, the rest is merely a matter of intelligence. At all events, I had to learn how to be proficient in the handling of many strange tools, because there was no one within reach to handle them for me. The experience was salutary for me in every way. It taught me to be ashamed of that kind of inefficiency which in towns is reckoned the hall-mark of gentility. It taught me the virtue of that independence which makes a man equal to his own needs. It also saved me from ennui. I found myself living a much busier life than I had ever lived. I had never worked so hard, and yet there was not a single part of my work that did not add to my delight. And I worked for direct results, for things I could see, and things which I might justly claim as my own, since I had created them.

I shall perhaps fall under the suspicion of morbid sensitiveness when I confess that I never took my weekly wage in London without a qualm and a compunction, for I could never make myself believe that I had really earned it. What had I done? I had simply performed a few arithmetical processes which any schoolboy might have done as well. My labour, such as it was, was absorbed instantly in the commercial operations of a great firm. I could not trace it, and I had no means of estimating its value. The money I took for it seemed therefore to come to me by a sort of legerdemain. That some one thought it worth while to pay me was ostensible proof that my work was really worth something; but so little able was I to penetrate the processes that resulted in this judgment, so vivid was the sense of some ingenious jugglery in the whole business, that I did not know whether I had been cheated or was a cheat, in living by a kind of labour that cost me so little. How different was my feeling now! At the end of an hour's spade-work, I saw something actually done, of which I was the indisputable author. When I laid down the saw and plane and hammer, and stretched my aching back, I saw something growing into shape, which I myself had created. There was no jugglery about this; there was immediate intimate relation between cause and effect. And thence I found a kind of joy in my work, which was new and exquisite to me. I stood upon my own feet, self-possessed, self-respecting, efficient for my own needs, and conscious of a definite part in the great rhythm of infinite toil which makes the universe. It is only when a man works for himself that this kind of joy is felt. So enamoured was I of this new joy, that had it been possible I would have possessed nothing that was not the direct result of my own labour. I would have liked to have spun the wool for my own clothes, and have tanned the leather for my own boots. I would have liked to grow the corn for my own bread, and have killed my own meat, as the savage or the primitive settler does. In this respect the savage or the primitive settler approaches much nearer the true ideal of human life than the civilised man, for the true ideal is that every man shall be efficient for his own needs, with as little dependence as possible on others.

Under natural conditions there is enough faculty in a man's ten fingers to supply his own needs, and all the avocations needful to life may meet under one hat. The familiar illustration of the number of men required to make a pin is typical of that contemptible futility to which what is called civilisation reduces men by mere dispersal of labour. Such dispersal develops single faculties, but paralyses men. It is like developing some single part of the human organism, such as a finger-tip, to high sensitiveness, by drawing away the sensitiveness from all the rest. To do this reduces life to barrenness; it makes it meagre in energy and pleasure; it makes work a disease. But in such a life as I now lived, it was not a finger-tip that worked but the whole man. The cabbage I cut for dinner was fashioned from my own substance, for my sweat had nourished it. The butter I ate was part of my own energy, spent over the churn, come back to me in the freshness and firmness of edible gold. My bread was baked in a flame kindled at my own heart [Transcriber's note: hearth?], and it was the sweeter for it. When I lay down at night I was quits with Nature. I had paid so much energy into her bank, and had a right to the dividend of rest she gave me.

Apart from all other things, the economy of this mode of life will be at once perceived. My expenses sank steadily month by month. I made a good many mistakes, of course, for there is more than meets the eye in remunerative gardening, chicken farming, and bee-keeping, as there is in most human occupations which appear delusively simple. It took me some time to rectify these mistakes, but before a year had passed I found myself raising all my own garden produce, well supplied with eggs and poultry for my own table, and able to earn a little by the sale of my superfluous stock. Some articles, such as coal, were excessively dear; but then, as a set-off, I could have all the wood I required for next to nothing, and we burned more wood than coal. Groceries I purchased in wholesale quantities from a Manchester store, so that in spite of carriage I paid less for them than I had paid in London, and secured the best quality. My trout rod served my breakfast table, and my gun brought me many a dinner. In short, I found that small as was the sum of money which I had earned, yet it was more than enough for my needs.

Winter is, of course, the trying time for a resident in the country. About the beginning of December the weather broke, and there was a week of driving rain. A fortnight of grey weather followed, and then came three days of heavy snow. From the moment that the snow ceased winter became delightful. No words of mine can describe the glory of these winter days. It is only of late years that people have discovered that Switzerland is infinitely more beautiful in winter than in summer; some day they will discover the same truth about the Lake District. It happened one day in midwinter that business took me as far as Keswick, and I shall never forget the astonishment and delight of that visit. Skiddaw was a pure snow mountain, a miniature Mont Blanc; Derwentwater was blue as polished steel, covered with ice so clear that it was everywhere transparent; the woods were plumed with snow, and over all shone the sun of June, and the keen air tingled in the veins like wine. Beside the road the drifts ran high, hollowed by the wind into a hundred curves and cavities, and in each the reflected light made a tapestry of delicate violet and rose. Those who imagine that snow is only white—dead, cold white—have never seen the pure new-fallen snow, when the stricture of the frost begins to bind it; such snow has every colour of the rainbow in it, and where it is beaten fine it is like a dust of diamonds. Under a hard grey sky snow appears dead white; but under such a sun as this it glowed and sparkled with all the glories of an ice cave. And then came the sunset, a sunset to be dreamed of. Skiddaw was a pyramid of rosy flame; great saffron seas of light lay over the Catbells, the immense shoulders of Borrowdale were purple, and the lake was truly a sea of glass and fire. Nor was this a singular and unmatched day. For a whole month the pageant of the snow lasted. Close to my own door were glories scarcely inferior to those of Borrowdale and Derwentwater. The glen was rich with all the fantastic arabesque of the frost, the moor was like a frozen sea, and four miles away lay Buttermere, ringing from morn to night with the sound of skates. There is no greater error than to suppose winter a drear and joyless season in the country. It has delights of its own unimagined by the townsman, to whom winter means burst pipes and slushy streets, and snow that is soiled even as it falls. But among mountains winter has its own incomparable glories, and holds a pageant not inferior to summer's.

But even in days of rain life had its pleasures. However bad the weather might be there were few days when we could not be abroad for some hours, and none when the mountains had not some peculiar beauty to reveal. At the end of a day of rain there were often splendid half-hours, just before sunset, when the mountains glowed with richest colour; when through the rift of thinning clouds some vast peak named like a torch, and the mist blew out like purple banners, and the watercourses sparkled like ropes of brilliants hung on the scarred rocks, and the air was fresh and fragrant with all the perfume of health. Fog we seldom had, and when it came, it rarely lasted beyond midday. And then there were the warm delights of winter evenings, when the wood fire blazed upon the hearth, and the gale roared against the windows.

I have already remarked that books read in the solitude of the country always make a deeper impression on my mind than books read in the uneasy leisure of towns. I found this doubly true when I came to live in the country. I came to my books with a keener and healthier brain. The great masters of literature resumed their sway over me; Scott, Shakespeare, Cervantes, long-neglected, took powerful hold upon my mind. It is not to dwellers in the town that great writers ever make their full appeal. They are too occupied with the trivial dramas of life among a crowd, too disturbed by the eddy and rush of the life around them. But for the dweller in solitude these great writers erect a theatre, which is the only theatre he knows. He is able to attend to the drama presented to him, and to be absorbed by it. He discusses the actors and their doings as though they were real personages. Effie Deans and Varley, Ophelia and Don Quixote, were for us creatures whom we knew. It was the same with later writers. Byron's poetry once more appealed to me by its revolutionary note, Shelley was interpreted afresh to me by these mountains which he would have loved. One incident I recollect which may serve to illustrate this new hold which imaginative literature took upon me. I opened one evening *Great Expectations*, and began to read it aloud. The next morning, at five o'clock, my two boys were contending for the book. For a month Pip sat beside our hearth, and Joe Gargery winked at us, and 'that ass' Pumblechook mouthed his solemn platitudes. We were continually reminding each other never to forget 'them as brought us up by hand.' Could any book have laid hold of us after this fashion if it had been read in the hurried leisure of a city life? It was the very absence of incident in our quiet lives that made these imaginary incidents delightful. We lingered over the books we read, extracting from them all their charm, all their wisdom, and there was more good talk, more discriminating criticism heard in my cottage in a month than would be heard in a London drawing-room in a year. And the explanation is simple. We had no trivialities to talk about; none of those odds and ends of gossip that do duty for conversation in cities; and thus such talk as we had concerned itself with real thoughts, and the thoughts of wise men and great writers.

One of the principal occupations of my first winter was the education of my boys. After the approved modern fashion I had intrusted this task to others, upon the foolish assumption that what I paid heavily for must needs be of some value. I discovered my delusion the moment I came to look into the matter for myself. I found that they knew nothing perfectly: certain things they had learned by rote, and could recite with some exactitude, but of the reasons and principles that underlie all real knowledge they knew nothing. I believe this to be characteristic of almost all modern education, especially since competitive examinations have set the pace. The brain is gorged with crude masses of undigested fact, which it has no power to assimilate. Fragments of knowledge are lodged in the mind, but the mind is not taught to co-ordinate its knowledge, or, in other words, to think and reason. The yearly examination papers of public schools and universities afford ample and often amusing illustrations of this condition of things. I remember an Oxford tutor, who set papers for a certain Theological College, telling me that one year he put this question: 'Give some account of the life of Mary, the mother of our Lord.' This was a question which obviously required some power of synthesis, some exercise of thought and skill in narrative. One bright youth, after a feeble sentence or two in which the name of Mary was at least included, went on to say, 'At this point it may not be out of place to give a list of the kings of Israel.' Here was something he did know, and it was something not worth knowing. I found that my boys had been educated on much the same principle. They could do a simple problem of mathematics after a fashion; that is, they could recite it; but it had never once been suggested to them as an exercise of reason. It was the same with history; they could recite dates and facts, but they had no perception of principles. It may be imagined that I had to go to school again myself before I could attempt to instruct them. I had to take down again my long disused Virgil and Cicero, and work through many a forgotten passage. At first the task was distasteful enough, but it soon became fascinating. My love of the classics revived. I began to read Homer and Thucydides, Tacitus and Lucretius, for my own pleasure. It was delightful to observe what interest my boys took in Virgil, as soon as they discovered that Virgil was not a mere task-book, but poetry of the noblest order. By avoiding all idea of mere unintelligent task-work, I soon got them to take a real interest in their work, until at last they came to anticipate the hour of these common studies. I took care also to never make the burden of study oppressive. Two hours of real study is as much as a young boy can bear at a time. He should rise from his task, not with an exhausted, but with a fresh and quickened, mind. On very fine days it was understood that no books should be opened. Such days were spent in fishing, in mountain-climbing, or in long cycling excursions, and the store of health laid up by these days gave new vigour to the mind when the work of education was resumed.

When the summer came on, life became a daily lyric of delight. By five in the morning, sometimes by four, we were out fishing. In the narrow part of the glen there was a place where the rocks met in a wild miniature gorge, and through them the water poured into a large circular rock-basin, about forty feet in diameter. This was our bathing-pool, and the cool shock and thrill of those exquisitely pure and flowing waters runs along my nerves still as I write. We often spent more than an hour there in the early morning, swimming from side to side of our natural bath, diving off a rock which rose almost in the centre of the pool, passing to and fro under the cascade, or sitting out in the sun, till sheer hunger drove us home to breakfast. Writers who boast a sort of finical superiority will no doubt disdain these barbarian delights, and wonder that memory should be persistent over mere physical sensations. But I am not sure that these physical sensations are not recollected with more acuteness than mental ones, and there is no just reason why they should be despised. I have forgotten a good many aesthetic pleasures which at the time gave me keen delight—some phrase in oratory, some movement in concerted music, and such like—but I never forget the sensation of wind blowing over my bare flesh as I coasted down a long mountain road on a broiling day in August, nor the poignant thrill of that rushing water in my morning bathes. And mixed with it all is the aromatic scent of the pines beside the stream, the freshness of the meadows, and the song of falling water. Sometimes, when the river was in summer flood, there was just that spice of danger in our bathing which gave it a memorable piquancy. On such occasions we had to use skill and coolness to avoid disaster; we were tossed about the boiling water like bubbles; incredible masses of water flowed over us, warm and strong, in a few seconds, and we came out of the roaring pool so beaten and thrashed by the violence of the stream that every nerve quivered. Breakfast was a great occasion after these adventures. Then came a stroll round our small estate, and an hour or so over books. Matthew Arnold's *Thyrsis* was a favourite poem with us all on these mornings. It breathed the very spirit of the life we lived, but for its sadness—this we did not feel. But we did appreciate its wonderfully exact and beautiful interpretation of Nature, and we had but to look around us to see the very picture Arnold painted when he wrote:

> Soon will the high midsummer pomps come on,
> Soon will the musk carnations break and swell,
> Soon shall we have gold-dusted snapdragon,
> Sweetwilliam with his homely cottage smell,
> And stocks in fragrant blow:
> Roses that down the alley shine afar,
> And open, jasmine-muffled lattices,
> And groups under the dreaming garden trees,
> And the full moon, and the white evening star.

Such was the life we lived. If we looked back at all to the life we had left, it was with that sort of sick horror which a prisoner may feel who has endured and survived a long term of imprisonment. It seemed to us that we had never really lived before. The past was a dream, and an evil dream. We had moved in a world of bad enchantment, like phantoms, barely conscious of ourselves. We had now recovered proprietorship in our own lives. Work, that had been a curse, was a blessing. Life, that had gone on maimed feet, was now virile in every part. This mere fulness of health was in itself ample compensation for the loss of a hundred artificial pleasures which we had once thought necessary to existence. We knew that we had found a delight in mere living which must remain wholly incredible to the tortured hosts that toil in cities; and we knew also that when at last we came to lie down with kings and conquerors in the house of sleep, we should carry with us fairer dreams than they ever knew amid all the tumult of their triumph.

CHAPTER X

NEIGHBOURSHIP

There is a wonderful passage in *Timon of Athens* which appears to express in a few strokes, at once broad and subtle, the picture and the ideal of a perfect city:

> Piety and fear,
> Religion to the gods, peace, justice, truth,
> Domestic awe, night-rest, and neighbourhood,
> Instruction, manners, mysteries, and trades,
> Degrees, observances, customs, and laws.

The congregated life of man, many-coloured, intricate, composed of numerous interwoven interests, was never painted with a higher skill. The word that is most expressive in this description is 'neighbourhood.' It strikes the note of cities. Uttering it, one is aware of the pleasant music of bustling streets, greetings in the market-place, whispered converse in the doorways, gay meetings and laughter, lighted squares and crowds, the touch of kind hands, evening meals and festivals, and all the reverberation of man's social voice. A man may grow sick for such scenes as a sailor grows sick with longing for the sea. There were times when this sickness came on me, this nostalgia of streets. It was only by degrees I came to see that neighbourhood has a significance apart from cities.

The first sensation of the man suddenly exiled from cities is a kind of bewildering homelessness in Nature. He is confronted with a spaciousness that knows no limit. He treads among voids. He experiences an almost unendurable sense of infinity. He can put a bound to nothing that he sees; it is a relief to the eye to come upon a wall or a hedge, or any kind of object that implies dimension. There is something awful in the glee or song of birds; it seems irrational that with wings so slight they should dare heights so profound. All sense of proportion seems lost. After being accustomed for many years to think of himself as in some sense a figure of importance in the universe, a man finds himself unimportant, insignificant, a little creature scarce perceptible a mile away. I came once upon some human bones lying exposed on the side of an old earthwork on the summit of a hill; heavy rains had loosened the soil, and there lay these painful relics in the cold eye of day. Two thousand years ago, or more, spears had clashed upon this hillside, living men had gone to final rest amid their blood; and it came upon me with a sense of insult how little man and all his battles counted for in the limitless arena of the world. The brute violence of winds and tempests had swept these hills for centuries; and he whose lordship of the world is so loudly trumpeted, had lain prone beneath this violence, unremembered even by his fellows. I understood in that moment that affecting doctrine of the nothingness of man, which coloured mediaeval thought so strangely: like the monk of the cloister I also had before me my *memento mori*. But in truth I did not need the bones of dead warriors to humble me; the mere space and stillness of the world sufficed. My ear ached for some sound more rational than the cry of blind winds, my eye for some narrower stage than this tremendous theatre, where an army might defile unnoticed. In such a mood the desire of neighbourship grows keen. One is cheered even by the comradeship of his own shadow. It becomes necessary to talk aloud merely to gain assurance that one lives. So ghost-like appears man's march across the fields of Time, that some active expression of physical sensation becomes imperative, in order to recover evidence of one's physical existence; and thrice welcome, like the violence offered to the half-drowned, is any kind of buffet which breaks the dream, and sets the nerves tingling in the certainty of contact with men who breathe and live.

The easy and ostensible remedy for such a state of mind is immediate retreat to the reassuring hum of cities: the more difficult but real remedy is the reassurance of one's own identity. Many people take the first course without admitting it; alleging the lack of intercourse or convenience in country life, whereas the real truth is that contact with the steadfast indifference of Nature has proved wounding to their egoism. A vain man cannot maintain his sense of self-importance in the centre of a vast moor, or amid the threatening bulk of giant hills. He looks upon nothing that respects him. He can find nothing subservient to him. Therefore he flies to the crowded haunts of men, and the porter touching his hat to him for a prospective twopence at the railway station, is the welcome confessor of his disallowed divinity. It is, alas! the most common and humbling feature of human nature that we all stiffen our backs with pride when the knee of some fellow-creature is crooked in homage to us, although that homage may be bought for twopence! No wonder that the man in whose character vanity is the chief essence cannot long endure contact with Nature; Nature respects no man, and laughs in the face of the strutting egoist. But if a man will live long enough with Nature to become reconciled to her impassivity, he begins to recover self-respect, by recovering the conviction of his own identity. He has that within himself which Nature has not, the faculty of consciousness. He is but a trifling atom in the scheme of things, but he is a thinking atom. He sees also that all living creatures have an identity of their own. Each goes about the scheme of life in deliberate wisdom. Why should he complain of insignificance when the bird, the flower, the horse that drags the plough, the beaver in the stream, the spider on the wall, make no complaint; each accomplishing its task as intently as though it were the one task the world wanted done? In the life of the merest insect are toils as great, and vicissitudes as tragic, as in the most heroic human life, and to see so much is to attach a new dignity to all kinds of life. The bird building its nest is doing precisely the same thing as the man who builds his house, and with an equal skill of architecture. The flower, fighting for its life, is engaged in the same struggle as man, for whom every breath and pulse-beat is a victory over forces that threaten his destruction. The world is full of identities, each unmoved by the tremendous scale of its environment. Hence a new kind of neighbourship is possible, wider and more catholic than the neighbourship between man and man. Kinship, not in kindred, but in universal life, becomes possible. There is no sense of loneliness in a country life after that discovery is made. The emptiest field is as populous as the thronged city. The Academy of God's art opens every spring upon the gemmed hillside. The building of a new metropolis as wonderful as London is going on beneath the thatch where the bees toil. All that constitutes human magnificence is seen to be but a part, and not a large part either, of a yet wider magnificence of effort and achievement; for of the flowers of the field we can say, 'Solomon in all his glory was not arrayed like one of these.'

The fact is that civilised man moves in a much too narrow range of affinities. He has forgotten the rock from which he was hewn, and the hole of the pit from which he was dug. He has reduced the keyboard of his sympathies by whole octaves. The habit of shutting up his body within walls, has produced the corresponding habit of shutting up his mind within walls. Hence Nature, which should be an object of delight to him, becomes a cause of terror or repugnance. Solitude, which is one of the most agreeable sensations of the natural man, is one of the most painful and alarming sensations of the civilised man. The civilised man needs to be born again that he may enter the kingdom of Nature; for to enter either the kingdom of grace or of Nature the same process is necessary—we must become as little children. Thoreau has described this experience in terms which might apply equally to the religious mystic or the Nature-lover. He tells us that for a brief period after he came to live in the woods he felt lonesome, and 'doubted if the near neighbourhood of man was not essential to a serene and healthy life. To be alone was something unpleasant. But I was at the same time conscious of a slight insanity in my mood, and seemed to foresee my recovery. In the midst of a gentle rain, while those thoughts prevailed, I was suddenly sensible of such sweet and beneficent society in Nature, in the very pattering of the drops, and in every sight and sound about my house, an infinite and unaccountable friendliness all at once like an atmosphere sustaining me, as made the fancied advantages of human neighbourhood insignificant, and I have never thought of them since. Every little pine-needle expanded and swelled with sympathy, and befriended me. I was so distinctly made aware of the presence of something kindred to me, even in scenes that we are accustomed to call wild and dreary, and also that the nearest of blood to me and humanest was not a person nor a villager, that I thought no place could ever be strange to me again.' This experience marked the rebirth of Thoreau, as truly as a new and delightful sensitiveness to a spiritual world marked the re-birth of Bunyan. The whole secret of re-birth lies in the recovery of lost affinities.

I do not recollect any particular crisis such as Thoreau describes, but I can trace the process in myself. I took no pains to cast the slough of cities; I registered no vows and consulted no teachers; it seemed that the thing was quietly done for me by the Higher Powers. I had no part in the matter except to be docile. Nature took me in hand, as sleep takes in hand the sick child; the only thing asked of me was my submission. The result soon appeared in the altered scale of my perceptions. I became indifferent to newspapers, to the doings and performances of public personages, to the rise and fall of literary reputations, and to a great many books which once interested me. I saw that a considerable number of those whom I had counted public teachers were no better than persons who talked in their sleep. They knew nothing of the elemental life of man, and were unfitted to pronounce verdicts upon his destiny. Novelists particularly offended me by their gross ignorance of life. The pictures of life they drew were as untrue as a description of a street-fight would be if written by a perfumed odalisque who had never crossed the threshold of a harem. The ancient elemental life of man, spent in storm and sunshine, under wide skies, they had not so much as looked at, and their voluminous chatter about man and his doings had as little relation to life as the philosophy that is enunciated in a monkey-house. Opera-bouffe performed upon Helvellyn would be a sorry spectacle; what was all this bedizened rout of people playing before the footlights of cities, but a vain burlesque at which Nature laughed? And as my sense of the importance of this kind of spectacle gradually sank, my appreciation of the serious drama conducted by Nature, upon a stage as old as time, whose footlights are the changeless planets, gradually rose. I had become the neighbour of Eternity, through neighbourship with things that are themselves eternal. I tasted the pleasure of enlarged existence, which had become possible through enlarged affinities. I had eaten of the Tree of Life, which grows wherever there is a Garden brought to beauty by the sweat of man's brow, and I had the knowledge of good and evil.

One form of neighbourship which brought me perpetual delight was—if I may so describe it—neighbourship with the stars. I had hitherto scarce given a thought to astronomy, save of the vaguest kind, and all I knew of it was derived from the recollection of one or two popular lectures. This was pardonable in a citizen, who is never able to see any considerable space of firmament. But when a man comes to live in the country he can scarce remain indifferent to a pageant so sublime as the midnight heavens. It is always with him; it obtrudes itself upon him; it becomes in time the scenery of his life. It pleased me on clear evenings before I slept to go out and take what I called a star-bath, a term justified by the real sense I had of waves of soft light and silence flowing over me, submerging and cleansing me, and setting my soul afloat. But very soon this purely aesthetic pleasure became also an excitement of the intellect. An immense curiosity seized me. I desired to penetrate this lighted labyrinth of space, to climb these shining terraces, to know where these vast roads led, in whose profound seclusion God Himself seemed to hide. In a very humble way I began the study of astronomy, and although I never got beyond its elements yet my whole life was incalculably enriched by what I learned. I sometimes felt that of all my neighbours the stars were the friendliest and wisest. That sense of insignificance, begotten by the pressure of immensity upon the spirit, of which so many men have written, I never felt; my most constant feeling was a kind of gladness which had its root in the conviction of some living friendly Power behind and in the spectacle. The sense of insignificance, if it came at all, was associated with the vanities of mankind. It did indeed seem a strange thing that a man whose thoughts could walk among the stars, should bend those thoughts to a mean eagerness for gold, a pride in dress, or the building of palaces, which when achieved are not so much as a single grain of dust upon an ant-hill. In a universe, whose arithmetic employs worlds for the ciphers of its reckoning, bigness as associated with man sounds ridiculous; and the biggest fortune or the biggest grief are alike infinitesimal. But when the desire of bigness passes from a man's mind, humility becomes pleasurable, and immensity is soothing. I forgot to think of the vastness of the stars; they were for me neighbourly and friendly presences, talking like a wise old nurse to me of things that happened before my birth, and the ancient kindness of Him whom a daring poet calls, 'My old neighbour—God!'

Neighbourship with the earth also became a vital pleasure and a source of peace. There was a time when I had a vivid horror of death; and as I look back, and analyse my sensations, I believe this horror was in large part the work of cities. It sprang from the constant vision of deformity, the presence of hospitals, newspaper narratives of tragic accidents, and the ghastly cheerfulness of metropolitan cemeteries. To die with a window open to the trampling of a clamorous, unconcerned street seemed a thing sordid and unendurable. To be whisked away in a plumed hearse to a grave dug out of the debris of a hundred forgotten graves was the climax of insult. It happened to me once to see a child buried in what was called a common grave. It was a grave which contained already half a dozen little coffins; it was a mere dust-bin of mortality, and it seemed so profane a place that no lustration of religion could give it sanctity. Dissolution met the mind there in more than its native horror; it had the superimposed horror of indecency and wilful outrage. But in the wide wholesome spaces of the world, and beneath the clean stars, death seems not undesirable. A country life gives one the pleasant sense of kinship with the earth. It is no longer an offence to know oneself of the earth earthy. I was so much engaged in the love and study of things whose life was brief that the thought of death became natural. I saw constantly in flowers and birds, and domestic creatures, the little round of life completed and relinquished without regret. I saw also how the aged peasant gathered up his feet and died, like a tired child falling asleep at the close of a long day. Death is in reality no more terrible than birth; but it is only the natural man who can so conceive it. He who lives in constant kinship with the earth will go to his rest on the earth's bosom without repugnance. I knew very well the place where I should be buried; it was beneath a clean turf kept sweet by mountain winds; and the place seemed desirable. Having come back by degrees to a life of entire kinship with the earth, having shared the seasons and the storms, it seemed but the final seal set upon this kinship, that I should dissolve quietly into the elements of things, to find perhaps my resurrection in the eternally renewed life of Nature.

Neighbourship meant also for me kinship, with every kind of life around me, and some friendly association with my fellow-men. The creatures we call dumb have a sure way of talking to us, if we will overcome their shyness and give them a chance. Moreover their habits, their method of life, their thoughts, are in themselves profoundly interesting. I seemed to have discovered a new universe when I first took to bee-culture. The geometry of the heavens is not more astonishing than the geometry of the beehive, nor is the architecture of the finest city built by man more intricate and masterly. Here, as in all things, we are deceived by bulk, counting a thing great merely because it is big; but if it come to deducing an Invisible Mind in the universe from the things that are visible, I would as soon base my argument on what goes on in a bee's brain, as on the harmonies of law manifested in the solar system. I believe we greatly err in underrating other forms of life than our own. The Hindu, who acknowledges a mystic sacredness in all forms of life, comes nearer the truth. Life for life, judged by proportion, plan, symmetry, delicacy of design and beauty of adjustment, man is a creature not a whit more wonderful than many forms of life which he crushes with a careless foot. The creature we call dumb is not dumb to its mates, and it is very likely our human modes of communication appear as absurd to the dog or horse as theirs do to us. We know what we think of the so-called dumb creatures; it might be a humbling surprise if we could know what the dumb creature thinks of us. The satire would not be upon one side, be sure of it.

To the townsman the simple dwellers on the soil seem almost as incapable of intercourse as the creatures of the field and pasture. Because they do not know the kind of things the townsman knows, they are supposed to know nothing. I have already said enough to show how absurd and insolent is this assumption. My neighbours were few, and simple-minded; but they possessed many kinds of skill necessary to their life, they had wisdom and virtue, and upon the whole a kind of fundamental dignity of nature. They were as shy as woodland creatures to a stranger's voice; they were highly sensitive to the mere shadow of a slight, and both suspicious and resentful of patronage; but they met trust with trust, and where they gave their trust they gave their full loyalty of friendship. In my youth, as I have said elsewhere, I often passed a whole day in a forest. I would choose some solitary glade, where my intrusion was audibly resented by the unseen creatures of the wood, who fled before me; but when an hour had passed, and the signal had run through the forest that I meant no harm, those scattered and astonished creatures reassembled. The whole life of the wood then went on before my eyes; the birds sang their best for me, the squirrel performed his innocent gymnastics with an eye to my applause, the very snake moved less shyly through the grass, as though the word had gone forth that I was a guest, who must be entertained and made to feel at home. This experience often recurred to me in my early days at Thornthwaite. It was some time before I was admitted to the free-masonry of the scanty social life around me; when at last I had paid my footing I found that here also was a commonwealth; here also might be found upon a narrow scale, but in authentic forms,

    Piety and fear,
Instruction, manners, mysteries, and trades,
Degrees, observances, customs, and laws.

CHAPTER XI

THE WOUNDS OF A FRIEND

Those who have been friendly enough to follow me so far in my little story will scarcely push their friendship so far that they will refrain from criticism upon myself and my doings. On one point, viz. the social morality of my conduct, I am so sure of criticism that I will anticipate it with self-criticism. Had I the moral right to desert the city, and to ignore the social obligations of the city, in order to find a life that was more pleasurable to myself? A city which presents a depressing variety of social needs can hardly afford to spare any good citizen, however humble, who is capable of social service, and for such a citizen to contract himself out of his obligations is very like skulking. I confess that this consideration occasioned me some uneasiness, and the questions which it raised have been treated with such admirable lucidity by a friend of mine, who still resides in London, that I will let him put the case against me.

The friend of whom I speak belongs to that class which may be roughly described as Earnest Good People. With very small means, and not much spare time at his disposal, he is nevertheless constantly engaged in what is called the work of Social Amelioration. The problems of city squalor, vice, and ignorance haunt him like a nightmare. When a very young man he made a voyage of discovery among the submerged tenth; got acquainted with tramps, night strollers, and wastrels on the Thames Embankment; slept in doss-houses and Salvation Army shelters; tried his hand on experimental philanthropy among the slums; and was driven half-frantic by what he saw. He has the makings of a saint in him; of a Francis of Assisi, of a Father Damien. He teaches in night-schools, conducts Penny Banks, and is grateful to any one who will introduce him to a desperate social enterprise which no one else will attempt. The first business of life, he is fond of saying, is not to get good, but to do good. Of pleasure, in the usual sense of the term, he knows nothing, and would grudge the expenditure of a sixpence upon himself as long as he knew a cadger or a decayed washerwoman who seemed to have a better claim to it. London is for him not a home, but a battlefield, and his spirit is the spirit of the soldier who dare not forsake his post.

Many years ago, when I was going for my summer holiday, he wrote me a reproachful poem, from which I quote a part, because it is the best index to his own character and the most lucid exposition of his own attitude to life which I can recall:

> The roar of the streets at their loudest
> Rises and falls like a tune;
> Midday in the heart of London,
> Midway in the month of June.
>
> And blue at the end of a valley
> I see the ocean gleam,
> And a voice like falling water
> Speaks to me thro' a dream.
>
> It calls, and it bids me follow;
> Ah, how the worn nerves thrill

At the vision of those green pastures
  And waters running still!

  But I dare not move nor follow,
  For out of the quivering heat
Another vision arises
  And darkens at my feet—

  White faces worn with the fever
  That crouches evermore
In the court and alley, and seizes
  The poor man at his door,

  Float up in my dream and call me,
  And cry, If Christ were here
He had not left us to perish
  In the fever-heat of the year!

  God knows how I yearn for the mountains
  And the river that runs between!
Ah, well, I can wait—and the pastures
  Of heaven are always green.

No one will question the nobility of sentiment in these simple lines, and they are the genuine expression of the man. In his case, however slight may be his claim to be called a poet, that hardest test of the poet is fulfilled:—

  The gods exact for song
To become what we sing.

It will be imagined that a man of this order would view my retreat from London with disfavour. He thought me guilty of a kind of social perfidy. No doubt the Earnest Good People, for whom I have the greatest reverence, will agree in the same verdict. A letter received during the last few days from my friend puts the case with such force, and yet with such good-feeling, that I will transcribe a part of it.

'I confess,' he writes, 'that the pleasures of life among the mountains leaves me cold. It is not that I am incapable of the same kind of pleasure, but, as you know, I have other ideas concerning the uses of life. I cannot enjoy sunsets while men and women are starving. The thought of all the misery of life for multitudes would, as Rossetti puts it, "make a goblin of the sun." You used to be very eloquent against good men who lived only for their own pleasure; are not you yourself living in the same way? I have heard you declaim against the gross selfishness of Goethe's aim in life—"to build the pyramid of his own intellectual culture"; are not you, in your own way, pursuing the same ideal? I have heard you say that nothing so belittled Goethe in your judgment as the fact that he was destitute of patriotism; he dwelt at ease among his books, while his country perished and felt no pang; and you live your joyous life among the hills, and have forgotten the Golgothas on which the poor of London endure their unpitied martyrdom. You are doing good to yourself, no doubt; but is it not a better thing to be doing good to others? I marvel that you can sleep at peace amid the wailing of the world. I cannot, and I thank God I cannot.

'What you do not seem to realise is that all our acts must be judged not only from the personal, but from the collective standpoint. Suppose all men followed your example, what would happen? Why, cities would soon become the mere refuse-heaps of the unfit. The drudges would remain, the captains of industry would be gone. There would be no leaven of higher intelligence left, no standard of manners, nothing that could set the rhythm of life. This is too much the case already. The merchant, the writer, the man of wealth and culture, live as far as they can from the struggling crowd. You would extend the process, and make it possible for the clerk as well as the merchant. If your new gospel of a return to Nature succeeds, we shall soon see the universal exodus of the best intellectual and physical units of the community. But you forget that some millions will remain behind, who cannot flee. Have you no obligations to these?

'Besides this, you do not seem to perceive that the ultimate drift of the new gospel is toward anarchy. The return to nature is practically a return to barbarism. You would have all men content so long as they grew enough potatoes for their daily needs. You would have England return to the conditions of the Saxon heptarchy. Each man would squat upon his clearing in the forest, ignobly independent, brutally content. There would be no longer that struggle for life which develops capacity, that urging onward of the flood of life which cuts for itself new channels, that passion for betterment which means progress. You save yourself from the collisions of life; but it is in such collisions that the finest fires are struck out of the heart of humanity. Again, I say, any course of action must be judged by its collective effect before it can be rightly understood. It is not the individual that counts, but the race. A good for the individual is not permissible unless it is a good also for the race. I do not admit that your new way of life is an entire good for you, for I believe you must in time suffer from your isolation; but even if I did admit it, I should deny your right to it, if in its large effects it means an ill for the race. Would you venture to say that the race would profit by it if your example were largely imitated? I think you dare not say so much, for you must be aware that the general desertion of cities would mean the decay of commerce and of the arts, the arrest of progress, and national disintegration. And if your own personal example would bear only evil fruit were it elevated to a law of life, it stands condemned.

'For my own part, I am where you left me. I am in the same rooms—dull, stuffy, inconvenient—you know all about them. I breathe quantities of bad air every day, and see a hundred things that distress me. I go three nights a week to the room in Lucraft's Row; struggle with the young barbarians of the slums, and am content if I see but a few signs of order evolving themselves out of chaos. A week ago I was knocked down by a ruffian, who came next day to apologise on the three-fold ground that he was drunk, that he did not know it was me he struck, and that if he had known he never would have done it. My ruffian was very penitent. He has since signed the pledge and is my firm friend. I chased him out of a public-house last night, and made him come home to my lodgings with me, where I gave him coffee, and sang songs to him. He followed all my movements with the big wistful eyes of a dog. There were tears in those eyes when he bade me good-night. He brushed them away with a dirty hand, and said, "I know I can keep straight now, sir, because you are my pal, and I ain't a-going against the wishes of my pal!" This morning he left a pineapple at the door for me—he is a coster, and pineapples are cheap just now. I felt more pleasure than I can say; I could have sung over my work all day, so glad was I. My dear fellow, don't think I speak pharisaically—you know me too well; but I do believe I got more genuine pleasure out of my experience with this rough fellow than you will ever get out of your sunsets. Lucraft's Row is a dull place enough, but when a ray of light does shine into it, it brings with it more than common joy.

'My objection to your new mode of life is that it is entirely self-centred. There is no projection of yourself into other lives. You are contributing nothing to the common stock of moral effort. You are simply marooned. It alters nothing that you have marooned yourself under conditions that please and content you. I think that if I were marooned upon the fairest island of the Southern Seas, where I had but to bask in the sunshine and stretch out my hand to find delightful food, there would be still something in my lot which I should find intolerable. I should spend my days upon the island's loftiest crag, watching for a sail. The thought of a thousand ships not far away, rushing round the globe, with throb of piston, crack of cordage, strain of timber, buffeting of waves, and shouting crews, would drive me distracted. What to me were blue skies and soft winds when I might be sharer in this elemental strife? How should I covet, in all this adorable and detested beauty of my solitary isle, the grey skies that looked on human effort, the violent wind, the roaring waves, the muscles cracking at the capstan, the strong exhilaration of peril, effort, conflict, and the glory of hourly contiguity with death! It was so Ulysses felt:

> How dull it is to pause, to make an end,
> To rust unburnished, not to shine in use.

> It was so he resolved

> To follow knowledge like a sinking star,
>   * * * * *
> To strive, to seek, to find, and not to yield.

You will not question that the sentiment is manly. Is there not then something that is unmanly in the opposite sentiment? Or, to be plain, my friend, is it not lack of courage which has driven you from us, lack of heroic temper, lack of that divine and primitive instinct which takes a "frolic welcome" in the "thunder and the sunshine," in the conflict and the stress of life?

'I believe that we are bound to be the losers by any wilful separation from our kind. This was the case with the mediaeval monks and ascetics; they lost far more than they gained from their separation from the common life of the people. It is the same still with very rich folk who are able to evade the harsh conscription of life; in evading the conscription of life they invariably deteriorate in physical and mental fibre. I can conceive nothing more ruinous to a young man than that he should have just enough money to make the toil for bread unnecessary. More lives have been spoiled by competence than by poverty; indeed, I doubt whether poverty has any effect at all upon a strong character, except as a stimulus to exertion. Life being what it is, we should take it as we find it: we gain nothing by going out of our way to find an easier path. The beaten road is safest. The man who boldly says, "Let me know the fulness of life; let me taste all that it has to present of vicissitude, joy, sorrow, labour, struggle; let me know all that common people endure, and endure with them; let me be no exception to the common rule, enjoy no special privilege, ask for no immunity from things harsh and disagreeable"—the man who thinks and acts thus is the man who gets the best and most out of life. But you, my friend, have simply copied the old monks in the arrangement of your life. There is nothing novel in your action, though just now your egoism is gratified by the sense of novelty and originality. You have simply gone out of the world to escape the evil of the world. You have bought yourself out of the conscription of life. You have yet to answer me one question: are you the better for it? That question cannot be answered in a day. Ten years hence you will be able to tell me something about it, and I shall be much surprised if you do not then report more of loss than gain. No man ever yet held aloof from his kind without paying the price in narrower sympathies, a narrower brain, and a narrower heart. The eternal spirit of Progress which works throughout the universe never fails to punish the deserter, and the most common punishment is atrophy. Not to submit to the process of evolution is to fall down the long slope of degeneracy.

'You do not need to be told that the entire history of nations confirms this rule. The greatest nations are those which have found life most difficult, and they have thriven on their difficulties. The soft climate, which reduces toil to a minimum, invariably means the enervated race. Under the harsh skies of Britain a great race has been trained to great exploits; but what part have the islands of the South Pacific ever played in human history? Give man a difficulty to overcome, and he at once puts forth his strength; difficulty is his spiritual gymnasium. Impose on him no need of exertion, and he will rot out, just as the races of the South Pacific are rotting out. I would measure the future of a man, or of a nation, by this simple test; do they habitually choose the easier or the harder path for themselves? The nation that chooses the hard path, that is not afraid of the burden of empire, that glories in the strife for primacy and is not afraid to pay the price of primacy in incredible exertion, in blood and sacrifice, is the nation that shall possess the earth. And is it not so with men? Here, again, I press home the need for considering one's actions in their collective aspect. Your course of life is easily imitable: would you have it imitated? There are thousands of men in London who could readily retire into a peaceful life to-morrow, on terms more favourable than yours. Every man possessed of a hundred pounds a year could do it. Yet there are plenty of old men, with ample fortunes, who never dream of doing it. They stick to their posts and they die at them. And it is by such men that the great machinery of social life, of commerce, of national progress is kept going.

'You would say, perhaps, that they are simply sacrificing the finer pleasures of life to the fanaticism of work; ah, but they are also sacrificing them for the good of the community. If the great surgeon or physician bolted from his duties the moment he had acquired money enough to buy a cottage, you would say he had no right to rob mankind of his skill and service to please himself. Have you that right? And if the whole nation acted in this spirit, how long would the nation hold its place of power and influence? In less than a century we should be as the Hottentots. We should be driven out before the advance of more energetic races, just as the Hottentots; who once possessed Southern Europe and Egypt, have been forced back into the African wilderness, where they live a life that is content with the gratification of the most primitive, the most bestial, wants. It is no excuse to say that the action of one man can have but little influence upon the trend of life in a whole nation. The merest unit in the sum, the cipher even, has power to change the total. The strength of wisdom in the majority of a nation may be more than sufficient to-day to counteract the folly of the unit; but there is always the chance that the folly of the individual may in time prevail against the experience of the wise, and pervert the nation. At all events, we ought to consider such possibilities before we hold ourselves free to do as we please in contempt of general custom.

'Do not be angry with me when I say that to me your flight from London appears only an illustration of that cowardice about life which is so common to-day. Men are very much afraid of life to-day; afraid of its responsibilities and duties; afraid of marriage and the burden of children; and not alone for the old are there fears in the way, but even the young men faint and grow weary.

'I can understand Stevenson flying to the South Seas; it was part of his prolonged duel with death. But his heart was in the Highlands, and could he have chosen, his feet would have trodden to old age the grey streets of Edinburgh. Your flight is altogether different. You have no real excuse in ill-health. You have simply fallen sick with a distaste for cities. You have had a bad dream, and you are frightened. I love you still; I count you friend still; but I cannot call you brave.

CHAPTER XII

AM I RIGHT?

I have given myself a week to think over the letter of my friend, and I am now able to perceive that it is built upon a number of most ingenious fallacies. The chief fallacy appears to be this—that he insists that the race must always count for more than the individual, and that the individual must fall in line and step with the average conventions of the race at the expense of his own well-being, or be judged a deserter and a recreant.

It is hardly necessary to point out that no doctrine could be more hostile to collective progress, because progress is not a collective movement, but the movement of great individuals who drag the race after them. I do not recollect a single human reform that has been spontaneously generated in the heart of society itself; it has always had its beginnings in the hearts of individuals. Thus the Reformation is practically Martin Luther, the Evangelical revival is Wesley, the Oxford Movement is Newman, Free Trade is Cobden, and so on through a hundred regenerations of thought, morals, and politics. 'The world being what it is, we must take it as we find it,' is a note of quiet desperation. It is precisely because the Providence of History has again and again raised up men who were incapable of taking the world as they found it, that regenerations and reformations of society have occurred at all. Society never moves forward except when it is goaded by the spirit of individual genius. So far as we can trace the history of civilisation, and thanks to modern research we have about ten thousand years to go by, civilisation is a succession of waves, each flowing a little higher than its predecessor, with an ebb between each. At what point is the ebb checked, at what point does the fuller wave begin to flow? Always with the advent of individual genius. A great man rises who founds a dynasty; a great thinker, who publishes new truths; a great lawgiver or statesman, who establishes a new social system. New worlds need a Columbus, and the social Columbus is always a man with sufficient daring to stand by original convictions. Therefore I say that human progress is only made possible by not taking the world as we find it; and that he is the best friend of collective progress who is the most obedient not to collective convention, but to individual insight.

I observe that my friend does not live in the spirit of his own axiom: else, why should he trouble himself over the inhabitants of Lucraft's Row? He is certainly not taking the world as he finds it when he devotes his hours of leisure to impart the elements of decency to gutter-snipes, and save drunkards from the pit. He is as much an individualist as I, only his individualism expresses itself in a different way; which confirms my original conjecture that we may be equally right in our own mode of life. Nor, by his own confession, does he really sacrifice his inclinations in his mode of life; he gratifies his sense of altruism in Lucraft's Row, and I my love of Nature in the solitude of lonely hills. The objects which give men pleasure may be so diverse that what is a source of joy to one man may be an equal source of misery to another. There can be no doubt that many of the martyrs and ascetics were honestly enamoured of pain and whatever credit they deserve for sacrifice, they pleased themselves by renouncing the world, as others by enjoying it; and all that can be said on the subject is that each pleased himself in his own way.

Thoreau's defence when he was accused of not doing good was that it did not agree with his constitution; and although the defence sounds like a piece of amusing cynicism, it was in reality a plea entirely just. The common fault of the Good Earnest People, as of most people, is that they can only conceive of doing good after a pattern which is congenial to themselves. But their mode of doing good, while it suits themselves admirably, may not suit every constitution, and people of a quite different mental constitution may be quite as good as themselves, although it is after a very different pattern. Thoreau did a vast amount of good by showing men, in his own example, that the simplest kind of life was compatible with the highest intellectual aims; would he, in the long-run, have served the world half as well had he forced himself to live amid the squalor of a New York slum? Are not we so much the wiser and stronger by the lessons taught in the hut beside Walden Pond, that it would be the poorest compensation for their loss to know that Thoreau by dint of effort made himself a fairly efficient city missionary, or pleased the pundits of a Charity Organisation Society? Or to take a yet more forcible example of my meaning: Hood wrote *The Song of the Shirt*, and Wordsworth *The Ode on Intimations of Immortality*; would either have gained by an exchange of lot? The one poem could only have been written by a man who knew 'the tragic heart of towns,' and the other by the man who knew the tranquil heart of Nature; but Hood, transported to Grasmere, would have written nothing, and Wordsworth in Fleet Street is unthinkable. As it was, Destiny took the matter in hand, and having men to work upon whose first principle of life was to fulfil and not to violate the instincts of their own nature, succeeded in producing two poets who served mankind each in a way not possible to the other.

I suspect there is a great deal of cant to be cleared out of the mind before we can become equitable judges of what doing good really means. I define doing good as the fulfilment of our best instincts and faculties for the best use of mankind; but I do not expect that the Good Earnest People will accept this definition. They would find it much too catholic, simply because they have learned to attach a specialised meaning to the phrase 'doing good,' which limits it to some form of active philanthropy. If they would but allow a wider vision of life to pass before the eye, they would see that there are many ways of doing good besides those which satisfy their own ideals. It is a singular thing that men find it very difficult to live lives of charity without cherishing uncharitable tempers towards those who do not live precisely as they themselves do. For instance, the busy philanthropist, nobly eager to bring a little happiness into the grey lives of the disinherited, often has the poorest opinion of artists and novelists, who appear to him to live useless lives. But when Turner paints a picture like the *Fighting Temeraire Towed to Her Last Berth*, which is destined to stir generous thoughts in multitudes of hearts long after his death: or when Scott writes novels which have increased the sum of human happiness for a century, is not each doing good of the rarest, highest, and most enduring kind? The fulfilment of one's best instincts and faculties, for the best use of mankind, is not only the completest, but also the only available form of philanthropy. Since Nature has chosen to endow us with diverse faculties, our service of mankind must be diverse too. In a word, doing good is a much larger business than the ordinary philanthropist imagines; it has many branches and a thousand forms; and they are not always doing the most who seem the busiest, nor do those accomplish most in the alleviation of human misery whose contact with it is the closest.

During the last year of my life in London I came into contact with a brilliant young Oxford man, who had manifest talents for oratory, leadership, and literature. He was in search of a career, and being a youth of quick sympathies and very generous instincts, he was soon caught in the tide of a certain social movement, whose chief aim was to induce persons of culture to live among the very poorest of the poor. The leader of this movement was a man of beautifully unselfish temper, but of no striking intellectual gifts; apart from a certain originality of character, which was the fruit of this unselfish temper, he was quite commonplace in mind, and could have aspired to no higher rank in life than an honourable place among the inferior clergy. He attracted this brilliant youth, however; a youth who had been president of the Oxford Union, and had taken a double first in classics, for whom distinction in life seemed inevitable. The end was that his convert joined what was really a lay order of social and religious service. He lived among the slums of Holborn, devoted himself to the instruction of the children of the gutter, kept the accounts of coal and blanket clubs, and accepted cheerfully all the drudgery of philanthropy among the poor. Most people, I am quite aware, will say that this is a very noble example of renunciation; so it is, and as such I can admire it. But is there nothing else to be considered? May not the sociologist ask whether a man is serving society in the best way by refusing to use his best gifts in the only direction in which they could have full play? For many years this youth had trained himself for a particular part in life which few could fill; he might have influenced the councils of his nation by his powers of debate, the mind of his nation by his gift of literature; he should have stood before kings and spoken to scholars; yet all these high utilities were extinguished in order that he might do something which a man with only a tenth part of his gifts might have done quite as well. Think of the picture; a scholar who never opens a book, an orator who addresses only costers and work-girls, a writer who writes nothing, a leader of men who exerts no public influence; and what is this wilful destruction of high faculties but social waste and robbery? No doubt he is doing good; but would not the good he might have done have been far wider, had he followed the line of his natural gifts, and occupied the place in life for which those gifts obviously fitted him?

This story is a pertinent example of the cant of Doing Good. By all means let those live among the poor and work for their betterment who have a distinct vocation for the task; but it is not a vocation for all. I object to the spectacle of a late president of the Oxford Union giving up his life to the management of coal and blanket clubs, just as I object to the spectacle of a thorough-bred racehorse harnessed to a dray. It is a waste of power. But the Good Earnest People never see this side of things, because they are afflicted with narrowness of vision. They admit no definition of doing good but their own. They cannot see that the man who passes from a distinguished University career to a distinguished public life may do more for the poor by his pen, by his power of awakening sympathy, by the opportunity that may be his to obtain the reversal of unjust laws or the establishment of good laws, than he ever could have done by living in a slum as the friend and helper of a small group of needy men and women. Decisive victories are won more often by lateral movements than by frontal attacks. The wave of force which travels on a circle may arrive with more thrilling impact on a point of contact than that which travels on a horizontal line. Society is best served after all by the fullest development of our best faculties; and whether we check this development from pious or selfish motives, the result is still the same; we have robbed society of its profit by us, which is the worst kind of evil which we can inflict on the community.

If this statement of social obligation is admitted as correct, most of my friend's strictures on my conduct dissolve into mere harmless rhetoric. For instance, he says I have 'marooned' myself, and goes on to draw a fancy picture of a South Sea Islander, content with laziness and sunshine, intimating that this is the kind of life which I have chosen. On the contrary my life is what most city men would call a hard life. I work hard every day, the only difference between my work and theirs being that my work is natural, wholesome, and pleasant, while theirs is drudgery. In what am I more selfish than the average citizen, who after all is doing just what I am doing, viz. working for his living? My friend would have me believe that the man who toils in cities does so from exalted motives. He is bearing the weight of empire, assisting in the growth of British commerce, and generally serving the cause of national progress, while I sit in ignoble independence on my own potato patch. I have known a good many men engaged in the lower ranks of commerce, but I have yet to meet one who is influenced in the least by these highly-coloured motives and ideals. They are intent on earning their living, no more. Their interest in commerce is precisely confined to what they can get out of it. They bear just as little of the burden of the Empire as the tax-gatherer will permit them. There is not one of them who would not object with vigour to take a single shilling less per week for the sake of progress, or any cause that might arrogate that title. Besides, it is surely a piece of undiluted Cockney egoism to suppose that the only persons who do their duty by the Empire are Londoners. We are still an agricultural country, and there are some millions of people who live upon the land. They do some kind of work, which one may suppose is of some utility and value to the nation; why should their kind of work be despised? They also pay taxes, give an equivalent of labour for their keep, rear children, educate them, and send them out to be of some service to the State; what does the dweller in cities do more than these? If I were disposed to argue the question, I should contend that the man who gets a bushel of corn or a sack of good potatoes out of the land has added a more real asset to the wealth of the community, and therefore deserves more praise from the commonwealth, than all the tribe of stockbrokers since the world began; for these lords of wealth, who reign supreme in cities, produce nothing. But since my friend is fond of quoting Browning, I also will quote him, and let the poet say in the flash of three lines what the dialectician would need a page to say:

> All service ranks the same with God,—
> God's puppets, best and worst,
> Are we: there is no last nor first,

Of course there is no disputing the general truth of the statement that nations are developed by the call made upon their energies by difficulty, and their power of response to that call. But why should such a statement be construed into a reproach on my mode of life? If my friend, who is probably sitting in a comfortable office at this moment, adding up figures which he could do almost with his eyes shut, would condescend to visit my potato patch, he would find call enough upon his energy. I have almost broken my back, and certainly blistered my hands, for the last four hours in hoeing my potato trenches into good level lines, and I have still an hour's work at weeding to do before I can satisfy myself that I have earned my dinner. I can assure him that bread-fruit does not grow on my land, nor am I in danger of being corrupted by a too easy means of subsistence. The worst crime that can be alleged against me is that I have changed my occupation in life, but I am very far from being unoccupied. The occupation which I now follow is the most ancient and most honourable in the world; I believe that Adam followed it. Is it not a curious irony upon civilisation, that it has so filled the mind with artificial estimates of work, that a form of work which is still practised by the great majority of the world's inhabitants is scarcely regarded as work at all by the insolent minority of mankind who happen to live in cities? But I have long observed that there is a universal tendency in men only to regard as work the peculiar sort of work which they themselves do; and so the artisan supposes he is the only genuine 'working man,' and the shopkeeper thinks the life of the professional man a piece of organised idleness, and the tradition appears ineradicable that all the clergy, from bishops downwards, never work at all because they do not sit in offices. It is of a piece with the theory of 'doing good'; for all men are bigots when they attempt to measure the universal life of men by their own little egoistic standards.

As to that imposing axiom, that all our actions must be measured by their collective effects, I heartily agree to it, because it is precisely here that I think my case is strongest. I do not, of course, invite all men to follow my example by returning to what my friend calls 'barbarism,' and there is so little danger of any such catastrophe that it is not worth while discussing it. But if any considerable number of men should think my example good, I would not deter them from following it, because I believe that no greater service could be done to society than to multiply the number of individuals who prefer a simple to an artificial existence, who are willing to live lives of honest labour and entire contentment, who will care not at all for riches, but will spend their utmost care upon their virtues, who will count 'self-possession,' the best of all possessions, and the power of living in God's world in cheerful happiness and modest usefulness the real programme of life which God has set before all His children, and which alone is worth our hope and struggle. The basis of all good citizenship is physical and moral health. Health is really wholeness, and so we get the word holiness, for all these words are products of the same idea. What service to the race can be greater, both in its present value and its ultimate effect, than to produce men and women both physically and morally whole? It is no doubt a duty to do all we can to help the unfit, and assist the infirm; but it is better wisdom and a truer duty to produce the fit and the whole. In the degree that I am better equipped as a man, I am better equipped as a member of the commonwealth. All questions of *doing* good are secondary to the question of *being* good; and to be good is but a synonym of moral wholeness. If a nation can succeed in producing efficient human creatures, efficient first of all in body, because that is the basis of all efficiency of mind, and will, and energy, there will be no question of efficient citizenship. As for me, I have found the means of a more efficient manhood by a return to a simple and a natural life; and therefore I am quite willing to submit my action to the test of collective example, believing that the more widely it is imitated, the better will it be for the happiness and well-being of my nation, and of the world.

The best way of doing good that I can devise is to make myself an efficient member of society; and it is obvious that if every man did this there would be very little work for the professional philanthropist. It is not help that men need most, but opportunity. Philanthropy is, for the most part, engaged in patching up the sick anaemic body of society; which is equivalent to minimising the distress of ill-health without producing good health. The wise physician knows very well that no amount of medicine will do much for the anaemic child; what the child wants is room to grow. We have social physicians in plenty, each with his own particular medicine, but all of them together have said nothing half so wise as these two lines of Walt Whitman:

> Now I see the secret of the making of the best persons;
> It is to grow in the open air, and to eat and sleep with the earth.

To create the best persons is to accomplish a service for society which is durable, and therefore is the only real good. I claim that this is what I have tried to do in my own case, and in no other way could I discharge my obligation to society so well. Economically considered I am now a profitable asset to society. I do a man's work every day, and I earn my keep. When the time comes for my children to go out into life they will take with them good thews and muscles, sound bodies, and well-furnished minds. I imagine that this is about as good a contribution to the cause of Progress, the service of Commerce, and the maintenance of Empire, as any one man can make.

CHAPTER XIII

THE CITY OF THE FUTURE

After four years' experiment in Quest of the Simple Life I am in a position to state certain conclusions, which are sufficiently authoritative with me to suggest that they may have some weight with my readers. These conclusions I will briefly recapitulate.

The chief discovery which I have made is that man may lead a perfectly honourable, sufficing, and even joyous existence upon a very small income. Money plays a part in human existence much less important than we suppose. The best boon that money can bestow upon us is independence. How much money do we need to secure independence? That must depend on the nature of our wants. Becky Sharp thought that virtue might be possible on 5000 pounds a year; and, apart from the question of whether money has anything to do with virtue at all, it is obvious that she put her figure absurdly high. Most of us put the figure at which independence may be purchased too high. If our idea of independence is the possession of an income that allows extravagance, if life would be intolerable to us without the gratification of many artificial wants, if our notion of a lodge in the wilderness is the

> Cottage, with a double coach-house,
> The pride that apes humility,

at which Coleridge sneered, then only a very few of us can ever hope for our emancipation. The first step toward independence is the limitation of our wants. We must be fed, clothed, and lodged in such a way that a self-respecting life is possible to us; when we have ascertained the figure at which this ideal can be realised, we have ascertained the price of independence.

My experiment I regard as successful, but there are two features in it which diminish its general application. One is that I took with me into my solitude certain tastes and aptitudes, which I may claim without the least egoism to be not altogether common. I had an intense love of Nature, a delight in physical exertion, and a vital interest in literature. I was thus provided with resources in myself. It would be the height of folly for a person wholly destitute of these aptitudes to venture upon such a life as mine. He would find the country unutterably wearisome, its pursuits a detestable form of drudgery, and the unoccupied hours of his life tedious beyond expression.

In reconsidering what I have written I perceive that unconsciously I have chronicled only the pleasant episodes of my existence. There is another picture that might be painted of mountains clothed in cloud, roads deep in mire, work done under drenching rains, early darkness, lack of neighbourship, isolation and monotony, a life separated by continents of silence from all the eager movement of the world. There are two pictures of the country, equally true; the country of Corot, idyllic, lovely, full of soft light and graceful form; the country of Millet, austere, harsh, bleak, impressive only by a certain gravity and grand severity. We all imagine that we could live in, and we all desire, the country of Corot. But could we live in the country of Millet? I confess that I could not have done so without resources in myself. It required a genuine pleasure in hard physical exercise to get through the duties of the day, and a genuine interest in literature to supply the place of those artificial forms of pleasure which relieve the tedium of towns. I do not know what I should have done without books in the long winter evenings. Nowhere is a 'city of the mind,' into which one can retire, so necessary as in the country. There is also needed an enduring and genuine delight in Nature and outdoor occupations, which creates its own sunshine under dreary skies. The mere sentiment of rusticity, created in the townsman's mind by pictures and novels, soon dissolves before the realities of a genuine country life. It is Millet, not Corot, who is the most frequent comrade of the man who looks for months together on the same expanse of fields, and moves upon the same unchanging round of labour. Therefore it is necessary to insist that no error could be greater than for a man with no real aptitude for a solitary life, and no resources of intellectual pleasure in himself, to attempt such an experiment as mine. He would weary of it in a month, and would flee, like a child afraid of the darkness, back to gaslit streets again, with reviling on his lips and bitter anger in his heart.

It must also be remembered that I did not go into the country with the intention of deriving my livelihood from the soil. My sources of income were separate from my mode of life; and although my income was at the best very small, yet it was sufficient to secure me ease of mind. I did indeed discover that the expenses of a simple life were slight, and that these expenses might be kept low by a moderate degree of industry in rural pursuits, but I never imagined that I could live altogether by the soil. I may frankly confess that while I believe it to be perfectly possible for a strong and handy man, accustomed to agricultural pursuits, to earn a living from the soil, my example has little to teach in this direction. The cry of 'Back to the Land' will be meaningless until general ownership in the land is made possible. It is the burden of rent, often a cruel and unjust rent, that has driven men from the land. Not far from me at Thornthwaite there resided a man and his wife who were among the most frugal and industrious persons I have ever met, yet they found it absolutely impossible to earn a living from the land simply because the conditions of their tenure were unreasonable. For thirteen acres of land, with a small farm-house and farm-buildings, they paid eighty pounds per annum, with an additional charge of thirty shillings a year for the right of a boat upon the lake. The most that they could do with this small holding was to graze four cows, and in a good season they got nearly enough hay to feed their cattle during the winter months; but with all the pinching in the world they went steadily behind at the rate of about forty pounds per annum. This is a concrete example of the difficulties of the small farmer, and it is sufficient to show how vain is the hope of any return to the land as long as rents are maintained at their present level. Were it possible for an English government to offer free grants of land as the Canadian government does, or even to fix rents and provide for the purchase of land as is the case in Ireland, multitudes of able-bodied men, wearied with the fierce struggle for bread in cities, would avail themselves of the opportunity; but under the present conditions of farm-tenure those who know the country best, know that, except in a very few districts, it is next to impossible to live by the land.

In these important respects, I admit that little can be deduced from my example. All that I can pretend to teach is that any man possessed of a small but secure income can live with ease and comfort in the country, where he would be condemned to a bitter struggle in a city; that a country life presents incomparable advantages of health and happiness; that it is not dull or monotonous to the man who has a genuine love of Nature, and some intellectual resources in himself; and that what are called the privations of such a life are inconsiderable compared with the real injuries endured by the man of small income, who earns his difficult bread in the fierce struggle of a city or a manufacturing town.

This leads me to a final question, viz. can nothing be done to regenerate our cities? Is it quite impossible that the City of the Future should be so contrived as to offer the best advantages of corporate and communal existence without those intolerable disadvantages which at present make the city a realm of 'dreadful night' to the poor, the weak, and the sensitive?

I began by saying that I am not a hater of cities. I feel their fascination, and four years of country life have not destroyed that fascination. When I had occasion recently to return to London for a week's visit, I was surprised to find with what eager joy I plunged into the labyrinth of lighted streets, how the blood began to quicken with the movement of the ceaseless crowd, how much of grandeur and beauty assailed the eye in the wide perspective of domes and towers and spires, how the very voice of London, sonorous and confused, like the noise of a great battlefield, thrilled the spirit, and I felt again that old and poignant charm of cities, that quickening of the imagination which lies in mere multitude, that perpetual seduction of the senses begotten by the revelation of so much effort and magnificence. There was an indescribable vivacity in this moving crowd, a contagious animation in the air; and, if truth be told, I found the air fresher and the sky less grey than I had fancied, for a south-west wind, soft as velvet and wet with sea-salt, blew through street and square, and the sky was full of sunshine and of racing clouds. I could not wonder at the love of cities; it seemed a passion inherent in modern man, fed and brought to its maturity by centuries of communal existence. And so the thought grew, that the temper of enduring antagonism to cities was a temper more and more impossible to modern man, who has long since left behind the realities of elemental life, the rude simplicities of patriarchal modes of existence. The City is with us, and it has come to stay. London grows vaster year by year, and there is no sign of arrest in its prodigious life. Is it then a dream quite impossible and vain, that cities may be so administered as to develop the best life of men, and not to stint it?

I believe that it is possible, and, most of all, by the expansion of the city area. There was a reason why men should be closely packed together in mediaeval times, when cities had their defensive walls against invaders, but those conditions have long since passed away. Entire security of life makes for the dispersal of population, and in a city like London, which has not been exposed to the perils of invasion for more than two centuries, there is no reason why people should be confined in narrow areas, From all that we can learn of the most ancient cities of the world, such as Nineveh and Babylon, we know that they covered enormous areas, although at no time were they secure from the capricious tragedies of war. Nineveh appears to have been a group of cities, united by a common government; cities of gardens and parks, so that the country flowed into the streets; cities in which the great temples, and palaces, and public buildings were not confined to any one quarter, but were scattered through the entire area of the city, giving an equal dignity to its every part. Let us apply the analogy to London. Let us suppose a reconstructed London, devised upon the broad principle of ample space and air according to population; of congregated and contiguous cities under a common government; of public buildings of utility and beauty equally distributed; and it is easy to imagine a London that should combine all the charm of the country with the advantages of the metropolis. The splendid streets, which are the main arteries of traffic, would remain, but the squalid tenements and alleys which are packed away behind them would disappear. A long chain of parks and gardens would unite the West and East, taking the place of a host of rotten rabbit-warrens, which are a disgrace to any civilised community. There would be no quarter of the town relinquished to the absolutely poor; Poplar would have its palaces of wealthy merchants as well as Kensington, St. Albans on the north, Reigate on the south, would mark the limits of the city, and all the intervening space would be filled with thriving colonies of Londoners, living in well-built houses with ample gardens. Manufactories would be distributed as well as mansions. The various trades would not be huddled together in narrow inconvenient corners of the metropolis; the factory, removed a dozen miles from Charing Cross, would take its workers with it, and become the nucleus of a new township. The artisan would thus work within sight of his house, and that entire dislocation of home-life, involved by present conditions of labour, would disappear. And each of these townships would have its baths, libraries, and technical schools, not dependent on local enterprise or generosity, but administered by a central body, composed of men of wide views and experience, who should deserve the great title of the City Fathers; and each would be saved from the narrow spirit of suburbanism by the proud sense of its corporate unity with London.

Such a London no doubt bears the aspect of a futile dream; yet it is worth while pointing out that in a dim and feeble way this has been the ideal after which London has been groping ever since the day when the population first overflowed its normal boundaries. The mischief has been that nothing has been done upon a grand scale and by organised effort. A bit of open space has been bought for a park here and there, while a much larger bit has passed into the builder's hands through local indifference or apathy. New suburbs have arisen in a day, not because any central power willed it, but simply by the combined greed, energy, and enterprise of the speculative builder, who invariably builds rotten houses, which he sells as fast as he can to guileless people with a passion for owning house-property. The result has been confusion, waste, and disappointment. The new township rises without any adequate provision for roads or railway accommodation. It is filled by a migratory population who do not realise these inconveniences or ignore them, as long as the novelty of the thing charms them; presently they move off again, a poorer population takes their place, rents drop, and another suburb is left to a precarious existence. I contend that this necessary expansion of the metropolis should not be left to caprice; it should be designed upon broad lines of development. The London County Council should buy up every acre of land that comes into the market within a thirty-five mile radius of Central London. It should be for the Council to decide whether such land as they acquired should be retained for parks and gardens, or utilised for building. It should be in their sole power to decide the kind of buildings that should be erected, and to bind themselves to erect buildings of public utility and convenience, such as libraries, baths, and concert-halls in a settled proportion to the number of dwelling-houses. At all costs the speculative builder should be eliminated. He is the worst sort of parasite on the community. His dishonesty is absolute, and the mischief which he works is little short of crime. Since the County Council has established its right to build houses, and has built them well, let it build all our houses, and give to other classes beside the artisan the advantage of substantial tenements. Let it borrow as many millions as it pleases; no one will complain if its administration is efficient; and after all, we may as well pay a fair rent to a central body, amenable to public opinion, as to a private individual whose own gain is the chief matter involved, We cannot do without the capitalist; but a Communal Capitalist is infinitely preferable to a private capitalist. Municipal Socialism is the watchword of the future; and instead of being jealous of the existing powers of the County Council, I would increase those powers tenfold; for without the widest kind of power, and even of despotic power, invested in some central authority, the chaotic expansion of London will go on to the enrichment of the few and the abiding injury of the many.

One of the greatest difficulties in this expansion of the area is the means of locomotion. It is at present in the power of a railway company, which is after all only a private trading concern, to create or ruin the prosperity of a suburb by the kind of provision which it makes for it necessities. A good, rapid, cheap, and frequent service of trains is a matter of the utmost importance to a suburb. But here again, our method of expansion is left to chance and haphazard. The speculative builder does not trouble himself about a train-service; he knows by experience that he can attract a population to any given locality, and he leaves the new residents to discover the inconveniences of the locality for themselves. It might be supposed that the railway company, in its own interest, would be quick to profit by the new population on its line of route; sometimes it does so, but in many instances it does not. One would suppose by the grudging way in which extra trains are put on to meet the needs of an increased population, that the railway company was a beneficent association, granting favours, instead of a trading concern in search of new business. The only real remedy for this kind of evil is that all the means of locomotion within a twenty-five miles radius of Charing Cross should be in the hands of one central authority. If a County Council is capable of superintending a tramway system, it should also be capable of superintending the suburban railway system for the public good. And if it be thought much too vast an undertaking for the County Council to become the proprietor of all the suburban lines, it should at least be in the power of the Council to exercise effective control over their working, and to compel the companies to make adequate provision for the outlying populations.

But it is clear that if factories and businesses were removed into suburban districts, carrying their armies of workers with them, a good part of the difficulty of locomotion would soon settle itself. It is the enormous daily flow of population toward the centre that chokes the channels of locomotion, and the wisest method of checking this flow is to make it unnecessary, by establishing manufacturing colonies, on the pattern of Mr. Ellis Lever's and Mr. Cadbury's colonies at Port Sunlight and Bourneville. There would still remain the difficulty of locomotion in the central districts, but with proper enterprise, organisation, and control, this difficulty is not insuperable. In a few years we shall look back with wonder and pity to the days when the infrequent 'bus, the slow and tedious horse-tram, and the exorbitant cab were the means of locomotion in which a city of six million people put its trust. The electric tram, clean, frequent, and rapid, will be everywhere; the electric cab will run at a normal fare of threepence a mile; perhaps also there will be electric overhead railways, constructed upon a system which does not interfere with the perspective of the main thoroughfares, for the overhead electric railway, whatever may be its defects, is a means of locomotion vastly preferable to the unventilated tubes on which we now pride ourselves. May we not also hope that the general application of electric force will do much to cleanse our atmosphere? With houses lit and warmed by electricity, factories run by electric force, cooking done in electric ovens, the vile smoke which darkens and destroys the city would disappear. The skies of London would be as pure as the sky of the Orkneys, and a hundred trees and plants, which now perish at the first touch of the fog-fiend, would grow in our city parks and gardens as freely as they grow in Epping Forest. With a fleet of electric boats upon the Thames, running at one minute intervals, the Thames would once more become the river of pleasure, and a highway of popular traffic. There is no reason why these things should not be. All that is needed is that London, through its chosen representatives, should assume the full control of its own life; working out the scheme of its improvement by deliberate methods and upon a settled plan; compelling the obedience of all its citizens to a central authority, and intrusting to that authority the complete management of its affairs, not as a means of personal profit, but for the profit and the welfare of the whole community.

In the meantime much may be done by personal enterprise. Is there any real reason why groups of persons, whose employment is in the city, but whose hearts are in the country, should not found small colonies for themselves on the outskirts of London? Let a thousand householders combine themselves into a company; let them choose their own site, build their own houses; let them erect their own Church—one Church upon the broad basis of charity instead of dogma would suffice—elect their own managing committee, and set themselves to the creation of a true community. Let them possess their own electric plant for heating and lighting; let every house share the common convenience; and since domestic labour forms one of the chief difficulties to-day, let common dining-halls be erected for every hundred persons, where good and cheap meals could be provided, or from which such meals could be supplied to private houses, at the bare cost of their production. Let it be the aim of these communities to collect persons of not one trade or profession only, but persons of varied occupations to compose their citizenship, so that as many forms of human energy as might be possible should be represented, each contributing its own element to the common life. Let all the trades permitted in the little township be conducted on co-operative principles, and not for private gain. Let due provision be made for efficient education, for the cultivation of the arts, and for the proper means of pleasure. Would not such a combination of men and women represent the best ideal of a human community? And can we not see that in the mere economy of means and money the gain by such a system would be immense? Suppose the capitalised value of such a township, including the purchase of land, the erection of houses, draining, lighting, and so forth, were put at a million and a quarter sterling, which is a generous estimate, this would impose upon the individual house-holders no more than 40 pounds per annum, calculated at 4 per cent.; and besides this he would share in the great economy of co-operative trading. If this estimate be rejected as inadequate, it is easy to compute the cost by adding a burden of 10 pounds per annum to each house-holder for each quarter of a million expended; but even if the total charge reached 50 pounds or 60 pounds per annum for each householder, he would gain immensely in what he could get for his expenditure, compared with what he could get for the same money in crowded London. Such a scheme is simply the application of the principle of co-operation to communal life. It is not chimerical; if it seem so, it is simply because we are so ill-trained in morals that we are unwilling to act together in practical brotherhood. It is not impracticable; it might be achieved to-morrow if we were in earnest over it. There are hundreds of thoughtful men who have perceived its attractions, outlined its system, vaguely desired its benefits; are there not a thousand bold adventurers in London willing to bring their vague ideal to the test, and to make a practical experiment which, once successful, would alter the whole science of living, and go far to solve some of the most difficult problems of our time?

It is for such a movement that I wait. Free and glad as my life among the mountains has been, yet I am sensible that I am deprived of many elements of human intercourse, which are efficacious in the growth of thought and the widening of the mind. I count my deprivation light compared with the higher gains that are mine in the composure of my mind, the joy of animal vitality, the tranquil days that leave no bitterness and bring no discord, each joined to each in 'natural piety,' each inwoven into the calm rhythm of fulfilled desire and duty. But my pleasure is too little shared to be entirely satisfactory. I see that there are terms on which my happiness might be communicated; that there is a mode of life that should combine all the delight of human intercourse with the tranquillity of natural existence; that the choice does not lie, and ought not to lie, between the city and the desert; that it is only by the folly of man, only by his greed, and haste, and carelessness, and contempt for the communal principle, that such a choice is forced upon me. The Regenerated City will come in time, too late perhaps for me to enjoy it; but the City Colony or Commune may come at any time; and when it comes I will gladly be its conscript, I will earnestly labour for its welfare, I will humbly seek to promote its success, believing that in the degree that society exchanges individualism for co-operation, personal gain for common good, man will enter on the widening evolution of a real progress, and find the path that leads him to a truly Golden Age.

www.ingramcontent.com/pod-product-compliance
Lightning Source LLC
Chambersburg PA
CBHW080212040426
42333CB00043B/2553